GW00585308

30126 **01451702 0**

DAGGERS AND BAYONETS

DAGGERS AND BAYONETS
A History

DAGGERS AND BAYONETS

A History

by

LOGAN THOMPSON FSA. Scot

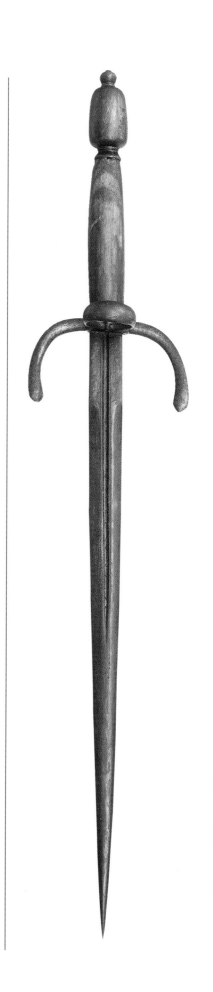

SPELLMOUNT
Staplehurst

Also by Logan Thompson
Guns in Colour
published by Cathay Books

British Library Cataloguing in Publication Data
A catalogue record for this book is available from the British Library

Copyright © Logan Thompson 1999

ISBN 1-86227-027-9

First published in the UK in 1999 by
Spellmount Limited
The Old Rectory
Staplehurst
Kent TN12 0AZ

1 3 5 7 9 8 6 4 2

The right of Logan Thompson to be identified as the author
of this work has been asserted by him in accordance with
the Copyright, Designs and Patents Act 1988

All rights reserved. No part of this publication may be reproduced,
stored in a retrieval system or transmitted in any form or by any means,
electronic, mechanical, photocopying or otherwise, without prior permission
in writing from Spellmount Limited, Publishers.

Typeset and designed by Louise Millar

Printed in Singapore

FL 11/99
623.441
045762

London Borough
of Enfield
Arts And Libraries

CONTENTS

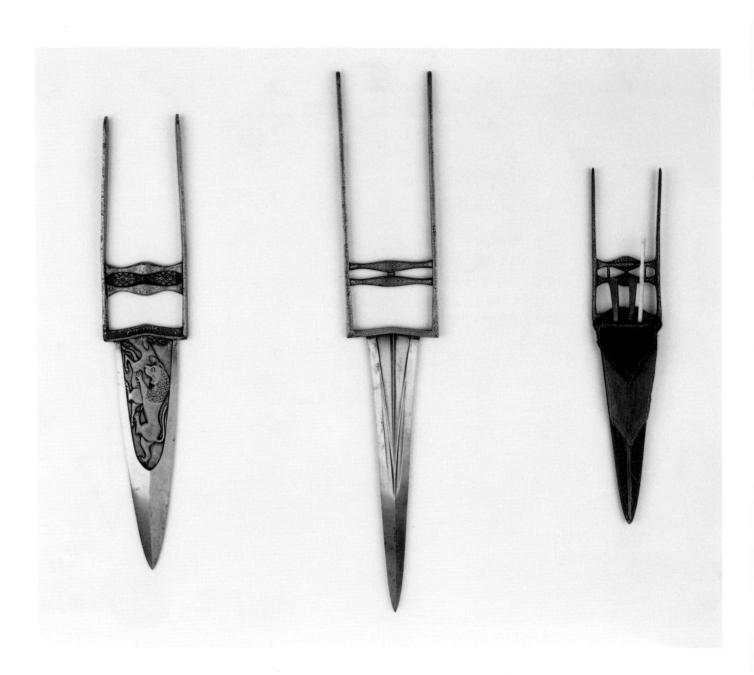

Left: 18th C Indian Katar.
Centre: 18th C Indian Katar with double-edged blade reinforced towards the point, the forte
with recessed panel on each side cut with three converging ridges, iron hilt damascened in gold
with panels of foliage, the linked baluster handles damascened with gold in geometric designs.
Length: 19⁵/₈ inches.
Right: 18th C Indian Katar, double-edged blade reinforced towards point, forte with a recessed panel
chiselled with lion attacking crocodile on one side and stag on the other. Iron hilt entirely gilt and
engraved with flowering foliage, baluster handles en suite, a panel with pierced foliage between.
Length: 16¹/₂ inches.

WITH KIND PERMISSION OF CHRISTIE, MANSON AND WOOD

Acknowledgements

To my wife Aneta, with gratitude for so much advice, practical assistance
and encouragement over many years, Mr D A Edge BA, DIP CONS. Armourer, Conservator
and Curator at the Wallace Collection, and Mr J Clark MA, FMA, FSA, Curator
(Saxon and Medieval) Department of Early London History
and Collections at The Museum of London, as without their help
the publication of this book would not have been possible.

Colour section picture acknowledgements

Plate 1 is reproduced by courtesy of the National Portrait Gallery, London.
Plates 2 to 8 are reproduced by kind permission of the Trustees,
The Wallace Collection, London

Roman civilian dagger plus sheath of 3rd century AD, discovered at Copthall Court. The blade is of iron. Overall length: 16.6 inches, sheath: 12.5 inches.
(NEG NO: 16501)
MUSEUM OF LONDON

GENERAL
INTRODUCTION

This book was written for readers with a general interest in history, students of military and social history, and to provide detailed technical reference guides for weapon collectors and military modellers. The book is in three parts: Part I describes the evolution and use of daggers in Europe from ancient times to the mid-18th century. Early daggers stemmed from the knife and are more appropriately known as fighting knives. During this long period its primary function was generally not as a weapon, although some patterns did possess particularly important military and self-defence roles, but as a useful tool for performing a variety of domestic, agricultural, and artisan tasks. Therefore, daggers were usually a dual-purpose item fulfilling functions of weapon and handy implement. We shall see how the arm also had a sartorial and social significance being carried as a means of displaying status. Dagger evolution and the numerous major category types and forms are set out comprehensively.

The purpose of Part II is to study the history of the bayonet weapon which developed from the dagger in the mid-17th century. This arm has continued in service until the present day. We shall see how it made an important and significant impact on military historical tactics, the composition of army units, and infantry soldiers' equipment. We analyse in detail the development and form of the specific bayonet categories and briefly study numerous patterns. Its battlefield combat use and the ways in which it contributed to victories will be studied. For some 200 years it was a significant military arm because of its influence in combat situations. A short history of firearms, upon which the bayonet was eventually attached, is included. The reasons for its long retention in service, even when bayonet importance declined after the introduction of rifled firearms (early in the 19th century) are examined. The advantage of its continued use today are also analysed.

For the benefit of general readers and collectors the book is profusely illustrated. The pictures, which are supported by captions, should better explain weapon patterns and assist with the identification of both daggers and bayonets. This will simplify a process which collectors sometimes find difficult. A list of other allied dagger and bayonet reference books, which the author has found particularly useful, is included for further study purposes.

Part III is wholly devoted to offering tips for collectors and advising on the techniques of purchasing, renovating, enhancing, and conserving daggers and bayonets.

Part I
THE DAGGER

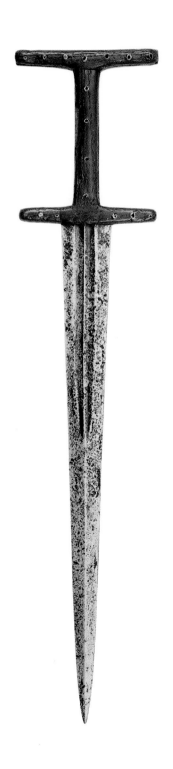

*Quillon daggers from
London, late 12th
century onwards.*
MUSEUM OF LONDON
(NEG NO: *830)*

Chapter I

DAGGERS IN ANCIENT TIMES

Early Evolution

Thousands of years ago, early peoples used very crude knives fashioned from wood, bone, stone and horn. 'They were designed for cutting and shaping wooden implements, scraping hides, preparing food and for other utilitarian purposes'[1]. As working techniques developed, flint was used to make slightly more sophisticated knives because being as hard as steel it could be fashioned to achieve sharp cutting edges. However, 'the fighting knife did not appear until the Stone Age was almost over'[2]. 'The blades of these early flint daggers extended up to a foot long and the hilts were made of material wrapped around a shouldered tang'[3]. Good quality knives were made in Egypt about 3000BC, and in Scandinavia from about 1800 to 1500BC. A material called quartzite, from which very good knives could be obtained, was present in Scandinavia. 'The earliest of the fine daggers that the Scandinavians produced from this fine material were long, slender, diamond shaped blades'[4]. Flint daggers sometimes had hilts of bone or ivory. Occasionally, these areas were highly decorated.

Eventually, metal was discovered which, being stronger and more flexible than stone, was used to fashion knives and daggers. This metal was copper, rich deposits of which were periodically found in the Middle East. Its problem was softness which meant that blades had to be fashioned in short and thick form in order to penetrate an opponent without bending. Subsequently it was realised that if another metal, such as tin, was added to

copper during the forging system, it created a harder alloy. This was bronze and its introduction was a technological achievement of great import. The new harder alloy was also easier to cast which made possible the fashioning of longer and narrower blades. With this tougher substance, stronger knives, daggers (often with double-edged blades), swords, and spear heads were made.

Sometimes, small quantities of iron were also used for making weapons because it was found in a pure state in meteors. The first ironsmiths utilised these lucky discoveries. 'Indeed, the ancient Sumerian word for iron was "heaven metal", and the Egyptians called it "black copper from the skies" '[5]. Such iron was being utilised in Egypt in about 3000BC. 'It was then found that beating and hammering some of the red and yellow earths that had previously been used to make paints would also make iron'[6]. The realisation that iron ore could be obtained from such deposits in the ground naturally much increased supplies of this valuable commodity. The main problem of the new material was that it produced wrought iron. This was obviously unsuitable for tools needing sharp cutting edges. However, a new smelting process was eventually discovered in which the iron was continuously beaten during the heating process. In this, the iron mass collected carbon from the charcoal fire, thus converting iron into a form of 'steely iron' which, when rapidly cooled in cold water, became harder. This discovery, coupled

Early Bronze Age daggers from the river Thames, 2000-1600BC. From left: copper-headed dagger with modern wooden handle; bone dagger; flint dagger; and modern reproduction of hafted flint dagger.
MUSEUM OF LONDON
(NEG NO: 18.848).

with greater sources of ore, led to much higher and better quality weapon production.

In about 400BC, the Celtic Tene culture created significant knife/dagger design changes. 'With this change, fewer and fewer double-edged daggers were made; single-edged knives predominated'[7]. One of these had a straight, heavy back up to which the single cutting edge curved to form a point. This pattern was the forerunner of the famous and important Scramasax.

It should be noted that bronze contin-

ued to be used in weapon making. This was because it could be fashioned more ornately than iron whilst conserving precious iron stocks. It was thus employed for dagger hilts and scabbards/sheaths. The Celts, with their renowned artistic attributes, fashioned the metal in most attractive stylised forms. In the Thames Valley, in Britain, Celts of the early 5th century BC imported iron from the Continent with which they made dagger blades whilst continuing to employ their own special skills in producing decorative bronze scabbards and hilts.

The Classical World

We now appreciate that metal knives and daggers were used by the Egyptians from at least 3000BC, and by the Sumerians from 2500BC. They were also used in the Mycenaean civilisation in about 1600BC. These bronze daggers had short tapering blades whose raised rib sections were finely embellished with a series of gold spirals. It was within the Hittite Empire around 1500BC 'that the first people known to have learned the technique of steeling iron were the smiths living in the Anatolian

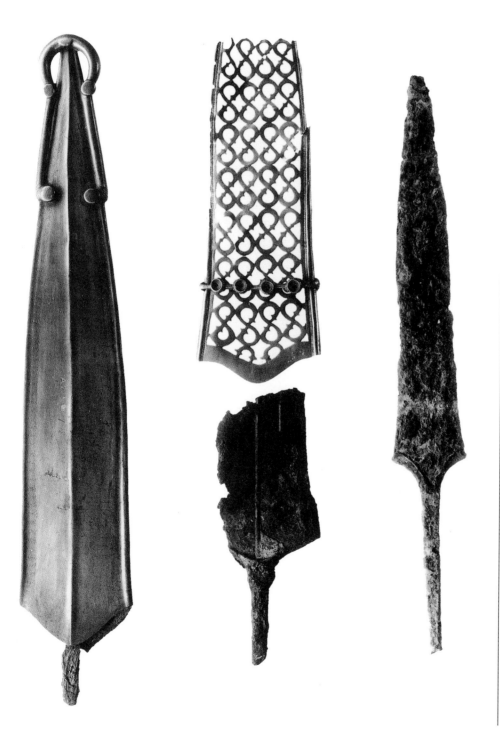

Celtic iron daggers with bronze sheaths probably of local manufacture in Britain discovered in the river Thames at Hammersmith. Early Iron Age, 4th C BC.
MUSEUM OF LONDON (NEG NO: 1955).

mountains'[8]. The ancient Greeks also carried them from the 5th century BC; a tombstone carving shows a Greek soldier trying to defend himself with his dagger against an attacker. The Etruscans often used daggers with slim iron blades of a shape rather similar to those of the later stilettos. It is interesting to note that the Romans did not adopt these though they had copied so many other customs of their more advanced and highly civilised neighbour. Instead, it seems they duplicated those made in Spain, in about 150BC, which had rather wide, V-shaped blades about 7 inches long with scabbards made from an inner core of wood covered with plated bronze.

From the last century BC, the dagger (*pugio*) was used by soldiers within the Roman Empire. This was initially rather similar in form to their sword (*gladius*). The grip was of wood, ivory or bone, and the leather scabbard often intricately decorated. Daggers had a double-edged blade curving equally on both sides to form a long tapering point. During the military reforms of Marius, which created a much more professional Roman army (104-101 BC), they were classified as an optional equipment item. 'Legionnaires also carried an iron dagger which, like the sword, was carried in a richly decorated scabbard'[9]. Soldiers were encouraged to adorn the hilts and scabbards in a smart and distinctive manner to inculcate personal and regimental pride. Doubtless, they undertook this morale-raising task enthusiastically because soldiers then, as now, relish opportunities to display personal pride and status. They were used as an emergency, last resort weapon and for administrative tasks. 'During the military reforms of Augustus, about AD18, the dagger became a standard equipment item'[10]. When the sword (*gladius*) blade was altered, in about AD70 to one of parallel sides and a short point, the *pugio* was unmodified.

Study of the one extant Roman soldier who died on the beach at Herculaneum, during the eruption of Vesuvius on 24-25 August AD79, revealed that: 'around his waist was a sword belt suspended from which was a sword in its scabbard and a second elaborate belt and scabbard for a dagger'[11]. Unfortunately, this was the only item missing. Perhaps, he was using it when the disaster first occurred, at about mid-day, and having collected his other equipment rushed out leaving it behind.

We should assume that Romans periodically used daggers for general purpose tasks. However, they probably carried them less after the population was prohibited by law from carrying weapons, in order to prevent civil violence, particularly during local elections. Subsequently, disagreements were, to a very large extent, resolved by litigation involving highly educated lawyers. They possessed, anyway, a very wide range of tools and implements for artisan purposes in farming, building, and house repair jobs. Therefore, perhaps, daggers were not much required for such tasks. Neither did they seem often to use them for eating. In upper class homes, at least, they used 'dishes, knives and spoons probably of silver. Forks were not used at table by the Romans. Meat was cut up in advance by a servant called the scissor'[12], then carried into the dining room.

Notes

1, 2, 4, 5, 6, 7, 8 Harold L Peterson, *Daggers & Fighting Knives of the Western World*, Herbert Jenkins, London.
3 Frederick Wilkinson, *Edged Weapons*, Guinness Signatures, London.
9 Keith Branigan, *Roman Britain*, Readers Digest Association Ltd.
10 John Warry, *Warfare in the Classical World*, Salamander Books Ltd.
11, 12 Joseph J Deiss, *Herculaneum*, Thames & Hudson.

Chapter II

THE ANGLO-SAXONS AND FRANKS

The weapons of the Germanic tribes who settled in Britain (firstly by invitation and then by conquest) just before and after the Romans departed in the early 5th century AD were generally remarkable for their simplicity. A few, however, were excellent as indicated by the remains discovered in the royal tomb at Sutton Hoo. These included a magnificent, sophisticated helmet and fine swords. For the great majority of Anglo-Saxon and Jute warriors, however, they were much simpler comprising only spears with iron heads of varying sizes set on a hazel or ash wooden staff, javelins, and round shields of lime wood boards. The latter had a large convex iron boss set at the centre of the outer side which provided a protective concave area on the inner side for the left hand. Swords were rather rare being only carried by kings, war-band lead-ers, and members of a chieftain's personal guard. These were long, two-edged broadswords, frequently of high quality made by slow, expensive pattern welding. They were highly effective in the close quarter infantry battle. The Kingston-upon-Thames Museum has three 5th-6th-century pattern-welded broadswords of the Migration period which are of the greatest interest. These are now the subject of detailed academic study.

Dagger usage was extremely limited. One is compelled to reflect on how warriors for the most part equipped in such a basic manner were capable of conquering so widely. Possibly, their determination, bravery, elan, and high morale more than compensated for generally inferior weapons.

The Franks and the Scramasax Dagger

The Franks, notable for their infantry traditions and the later creation of a large Empire under Charlemagne, were better and more diversely equipped than our Anglo-Saxon forebears. Amongst their ancillary weapons were the throwing axe (*francisca*) and the dagger. This was the Scramasax, eventually to become one of the most common Anglo-Saxon weapons for many centuries. The term 'Scramasax' is used to denote Frankish and other single-edged knives or cutlasses because of an oft quoted passage in Gregory of Tours, who, in his history of the Franks, speaks of: 'boys with strong knives (*cultris validis*) which they commonly call scramasaxes (*scramasaxos*) '[1]. Scramasax is actually a collective name for a very wide assortment of blade types ranging from about 2.5 feet long down to 3 inches. The author, who was privileged to re-classify the large reserve Scramasax collection in the Museum of London, was immediately struck by the profusion of pattern types, shapes and sizes. To standardise these it was decided to categorise those over 1 foot and 10 inches long as swords, examples under 7 inches as household utensils, and those in between as daggers. We concentrate here on the daggers.

Readers should not be confused by the term 'dagger', which tends to conjure up images of more delicate varieties used extensively in the 12th to 15th centuries, such as the Rondel and Ear daggers. There is little resemblance between those and the Scramasax. 'The scramasax proper, proper at least in archaeology, may best be described as a sort of clumsy carving knife, to which on the average its size likewise

approximates'[2]. These arms are all noticeable for their sturdiness, blade thickness, and heavy weight which is sometimes out of ratio to their length. But they provided both a sturdy all-purpose useful tool in the fields and the house and effective second line weapon. It was also found convenient in the commission of murky deeds; an authenticated reference states that: 'those who assassinated Sigibert in AD575 used scramsaxes!' Their use eventually spread from the Continental Franks to Britain in the 7th century. Thereafter, its use by the Anglo-Saxons rapidly became very widespread and remained so for about 400 years.

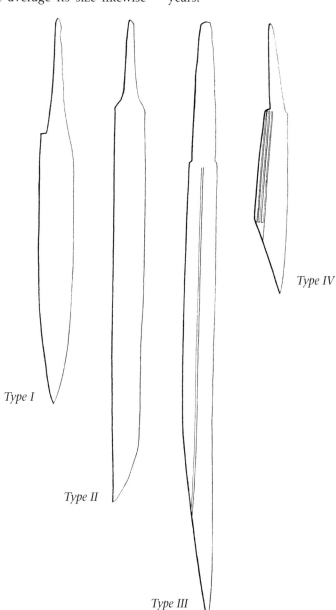

Type I

Type II

Type III

Type IV

Classification of Scramasax development.

I: Frankish type, late 6th-8th C

II: Norwegian type, 7th and 8th C

III Hurbuck type, 8th-10th C

IV Honey Lane type, 10th-11th C

MUSEUM OF LONDON CATALOGUE.

Development of Types

Because this particular dagger form was in use for so many centuries in Scandinavia, Gaul and England, its shape and appearance periodically changed. Readers' attention is directed to the diagram. It will be noted that there were four main types, but to these must be added numerous other forms resulting from transitional changes between categories. The Kingston Museum has an interesting example incorporating characteristics of both the Hurbuck and Honey Lane (London) types.

No. I. Frankish

Late 6th to 8th centuries. These were usually heavy, achieving maximum blade length of up to about 2 feet. The curved blade back and slightly upward curved cutting edge join to form the point. These were first made in Merovingian Gaul in the late 6th century. Some have been found in England dating from the early 7th century. They were rarely inscribed.

No. II. Norwegian

7th to 8th centuries. The most distinctive characteristic is the straight, flat blade top (sometimes rather concave in the centre). This type is common in Scandinavian patterns, and because their size was often considerable they were probably mostly used as swords.

No. III. Hurbuck

8th to 10th centuries. The name relates to a 9th-century hoard found at Hurbuck, in England. Note break of straight blade top stretching down at a gradual angle to form a very long blade point. They have deep, parallel lines etched below the blade top. They were often inscribed with copper, brass, or white metal. Many examples must have been swords.

No. IV. Honey Lane

10th to 11th centuries. Distinctive points to note: upward formed tang, very sharp obtuse downward angle of blade top joining the upward tilt of cutting blade to form sharp point. An example found in Honey Lane market was dated between 978 and 1016 by means of coins discovered with it. Many daggers of this type have tangs which extend parallel with the blade edges. These were carried in angular leather sheaths. 'Between this extreme form and the Hurbuck type are many transitional and cross-bred examples; but the scarcity of evidence as to date prevents us from arranging these in a reliable, evolutionary sequence'[3].

Group of Scramasax daggers from the Museum of London. The hilts, guards and pommels are all missing. (NEG NO: 244/1/1).

Manufacture

Scramasaxes were usually made of iron, some of steely iron and a few by the expensive pattern welding method. Dagger blades varied in length from about 7 to 15 inches. They invariably had only one cutting edge. Blade tops were particularly thick and robust contributing to the clumsy feel of the arm. They tended to be blade heavy. However, these shortcomings created combat advantages which we shall examine later. The tangs, the top narrow extension of the blade to which the hilt/handle was attached are rather short, further causing the weapon to be somewhat 'point heavy'. Type III was an exception to this trend. The guard was very small in a semicircular button shape. This is, perhaps, not surprising because in Britain in the Migration period Germanic broad swords were also usually fitted with small guards made of bone or hard wood. A few expensive Continental swords had short, straight, metal crossguards. Hilts were generally formed with semi-circular wooden cheek plates riveted to the tang sides then bound with leather and wire. Pommels, the bulbous semicircular cap at the end of the tang, prevented the weapon slipping out of the carrier's hand. They were also rather small. But there are exceptions. On some expensively produced Scramasax daggers these were much more pronounced, being of circular disk or 'cocked hat' form. Because the pommel could be seen by others it was frequently heavily enhanced with an elaborate adornment of inlaid brass, silver and sometimes even gold. So, this visible weapon area was an important one for demonstrating status. The top sections of high quality blades were also sometimes magnificently ornamented with inlaid decorated panels (see picture page 20). It appears that a few daggers were designed for hunting purposes. These had blades which curved upwards towards the tip. Presumably they were useful in the animal skinning process.

Scramasax daggers were carried in a leather sheath hanging against the left thigh. 'The weapon was suspended from the waist belt by means of a series of small bronze loops'[4]. Just such a specimen was discovered in a cemetery at Dunstable.

Honey Lane type dagger of the late 10th to 11th C. Example is slightly unusual lacking the customary incised lines at blade top.
MUSEUM OF LONDON
(NEG NO: 16132).

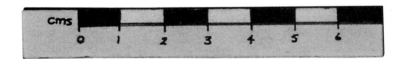

Honey Lane Scramasax dagger with intricately engraved and decorated blade. MUSEUM OF LONDON

Combat Use

The primary weapon of the Franks and Anglo-Saxons was the spear. This was not hurled at opponents (like javelins) because such action would naturally deprive a man of his main arm. The close-quarter melee of contemporary battles was a chaotic, disorganised and confusing area of numerous simultaneous man-to-man personal conflicts. A dangerous place to be! Shields provided vital protection against enemies' arms, whilst the spear was vigorously directed with overarm, or upward thrusts against any weakly guarded portions of an adversary. Such fighting was a period of stimulating, hazardous, adrenalin pumping struggle demanding great courage and guts. If the spear was broken, accidentally dropped, or became irretrievably embedded in an antagonist's shield or anatomy, the warrior was momentarily defenceless. He then resorted to using his Scramasax dagger, assuming that a discarded spear was not available which could be snatched up and used. Long bladed ones could be wielded in an overarm slashing, or hacking strokes, the heavy blade weight helping to cause percussive wounds. Its long pointed blade, reinforced by the very heavy blade-backing, also provided an ideal thrusting weapon guaranteed to penetrate contemporary protective clothing, or mail, causing deep fatal wounds.

The Anglo-Saxon Scramasax dagger was therefore a popular second line weapon for some four centuries. Its retention for such a long period was proof of its effectiveness and dependability. Apart from combat employment it was used in a multitude of other tasks such as carpentry, wood chopping, household repairs, and brush clearance on the farm. It was thus a versatile, useful and most practical multi-purpose item.

Notes

1, 3 R E M Wheeler, *London and the Saxons*, Museum of London catalogue.
2 A B Ward Perkins, *London and the Saxons*, Museum of London catalogue.
4 D M Wilson, *The Anglo-Saxons*, Thames & Hudson.

Chapter III

EARLY MEDIEVAL DAGGERS

1150-1550

Introduction

We shall now examine the daggers which were developed across Europe in the early Middle Ages. The Scramasax dagger continued in use until the 12th century in Scandinavia, France and England. This trend typifies the common conservative custom of retaining a trusted implement for a very long time; a practice most noticeable in the history of weapons. In 1066, the Scramasax dagger was used by the English at the battles of Fulford, Stamford Bridge and Hastings. It was subsequently retained as a general purpose tool. Thereafter, new dagger patterns, lighter and more sophisticated, were developed by various European nations. We shall study the most distinctive types. Readers should appreciate, however, that many dagger forms were also produced which cannot be categorised specifically into one of the most popular forms. Such a one, discovered in the River Thames two years ago, was seen by the author in the Museum of London. It was in remarkably good condition, dated at about AD1500, but could not be definitely categorised into one of the common forms. Such instances tend to cause slight confusion to collectors attempting to identify unusual examples. It is of interest that: 'fashions in design, however, spread quickly from country to country and it is very difficult to lay down any stylistic characteristics for any particular area'[1]. Daggers and knives were carried in sheaths, or scabbards, generally made of leather-covered wooden laths. Sometimes, these were made of hardened leather only.

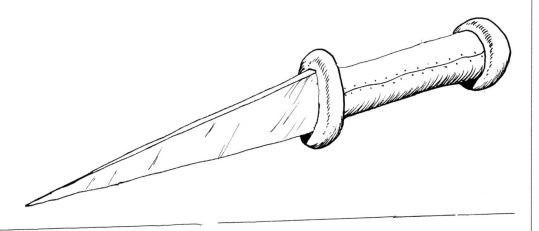

Drawing of a common form of knife dagger, c1400.
COURTESY OF D W WORTHY ESQ

Sources

Many old daggers have been discovered over the last 100 years and are, indeed, still being found regularly. Such occurrences are most exciting. They have enabled more detailed and credible research to be undertaken, resulting in the creation of accurate typology and categorisation.

Many weapons have been/are found in rivers or adjacent mud flats. One is compelled to ask why so many should have been lost in such areas. The answers give us an interesting insight into medieval life. At that time, in European cities based upon rivers, the most convenient form of transport was the boat. This was particularly so, for example, in Flemish towns such as Bruges with its busy, intricate canal system, and in London. In such places, many small craft provided the transport services undertaken today by buses, taxis and the underground. Personal items were therefore regularly lost in the water during such journeys, particularly at night, when passengers hopped in and out of the craft.

Ancient weapons are also often found in such places because early settlements were frequently established on river banks. Some weapons were, perhaps, deliberately broken/damaged before disposal for reasons we can only guess at. The author has handled some of these which often have sharply bent or broken blades. Maybe some had been officially confiscated from wrongdoers. Rivers functioned as waste disposal areas in medieval times which is very fortunate for modern historians! Weapons in ancient times were sometimes selected as votive offerings, for religious purposes, and thus cast upon specially significant waters. This could explain the discovery of some magnificent items recovered from the Thames, such as the bronze parade shield found at Battersea, and numerous bronze swords.

It should be appreciated that river bottom mud is generally a better weapon preservative than land soil, which is often acid and so more detrimental to metal. Certainly, the state of many examples excavated from the Thames, which were handled by the author, were in remarkably good condition considering their age.

Dagger Purposes

It is appropriate now to examine dagger purposes and therefore better understand why so many men carried them during the Middle Ages. Their basic roles were: as a multi-purpose tool, for personal defence, and when necessary an offensive weapon in war. In the contemporary unruly and rough times the possession of a weapon was, perhaps, an obvious means of deterring an attack. It was, of course, periodically used in the commission of crimes (as we shall see later) but these planned, deliberate assaults were few in relation to the number of daggers being commonly carried.

They were periodically used for eating, prompting us now to contemplate briefly the contemporary manner of dining. Forks had still not been invented, indeed, it was not until the 17th century that they were introduced, predictably by the French. Sometimes, the long, slender handles of spoons were used to spear a fragment of food and transfer it to the mouth. Eating methods usually equated in crudity to other daily mandatory functions all of which were conducted in disagreeable circumstances. To eat one used hands (normally unwashed), greasy pewter or wooden platters, and wooden spoons. If no other utensils, such as domestic knives were available, the dagger was used to cut food then sometimes transfer portions to the mouth with the tip. Soft foods, such as soup and vegetables, were eaten with the spoon. Any clothing stained with food remained blemished thereafter! The arm was also used for a variety of other tasks such as mending boots, house repairs, and farm jobs. The final function of the dagger was as an obvious and ostentatious means of enhancing a man's personal apparel, conforming to fashion which dictated that all men carried them. Therefore, nearly every male possessed one – rather like the tie today; people wear them on account of custom and because most other people do.

Those of senior status and wealth possessed daggers of high quality (usually pattern welded) which were frequently artistically and expensively decorated. It is of interest that such patterns were often copied, in an inexpensive and cruder manner, by those endeavouring to emulate the possessions and status of higher class persons. So, to a degree, daggers were a status symbol rather as expensive watches and their cheaper copies can be today.

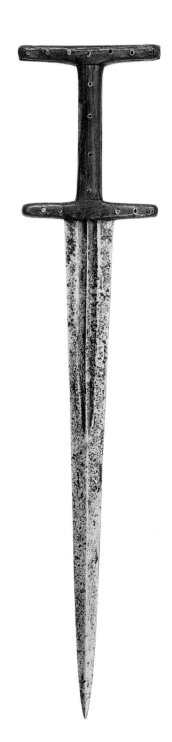

Dagger Types

We shall now consider in some detail the rather bewildering range of dagger forms in use from the late 12th century onwards. It will be realised that different types and forms of daggers were being used during the same period (as with swords) due to

the conservatism of some owners or because they were content with an existing old pattern. 'Generally speaking, seven major families of daggers appeared in western Europe between the late thirteenth century and AD1500'[2].

Knife Daggers 1150-1500

In the Middle Ages, a man carried a knife or dagger in his belt or suspended from it. 'The commonest type of civilian dagger in this period was the single-edged knife dagger, derived, with a greater or lesser degree of elaboration, from the ordinary domestic knife'[3]. Frequently these were made to fulfil the functions of a weapon and a domestic appliance, another example of how a household implement was adapted for weapon usage. This pattern was fashioned

in a neater, lighter manner than the Scramasax knife. The single-edged blade was triangular shaped in long and slender form. To the author, many bear a very close resemblance to contemporary Sabatier kitchen knives. Some medieval knives did have wider and more rounded blades. Hilts, usually of wood, were generally very simple with tiny round pommels. However, some rare examples from the late 15th century were more elaborate.

Military Influence Upon Daggers

By the middle of the 13th century events on the battlefield created a much more significant military role for the dagger. Since about 1120 the mounted, armoured knight had substantially increased his personal protection. This was achieved with better helmets (the rudimentary great helm), and by wearing more mail, and pieces of boiled leather on his elbows and knees. Even

small sections of plate armour had been adopted. He was thus far less vulnerable in battle. Consequently dagger designs were altered to overcome these better defences. Dual purpose models with long, stiff, tapering blades were introduced to penetrate gaps in the knights' armour by means of a direct, straight thrust. They could still, when appropriate, be used to make over-

Baselard dagger, possibly Italian or Swiss, 14th C. THE BOARD OF TRUSTEES OF THE ROYAL ARMOURIES (NEG NO: A5/984).

shoulder slashing strokes. Long military daggers were also designed to perform the same function of penetrating weaker portions of an opponent. Such daggers became an extra, standard equipment item for knights in about 1250.

During the 14th century it became fairly common for knights to fight on foot to strengthen the infantry defensive line. This necessitated greater dagger usage. At Agincourt (1415) archers used them to dispatch dismounted knights by thrusting the narrow blades through helmet vents and other apertures.

Dagger group from the Museum of London.
From left:

Military Quillon dagger with double-edged triangular formed blade. Note distinctive arrowhead shaped pommel.

Civilian Kidney/Ballock dagger of about 1450 with single-edged blade with maker's mark. Note overlarge scale of lobes forming the guard.

Rondel of about 1450 with long, tapering single-edged blade ideal for penetrating armour. Note matching guard and pommel of hexagonal plates, and the four tubular brass rivets which retained grip on tang, tang edge gilded and rilled diagonally. Blade length: 14.7 inches.

Rondel of late 15th C with single-edged blade and matching pommel and guard of round iron discs. Note: missing grip would not have been retained by rivets but with heavy braiding in spiral or horizontal form.

(NEG NO: 264)

Early Quillon Daggers: 1180-1450

Quillon daggers, like many Rondel patterns, were classed as a military weapon, unlike the knife dagger and most Ballock/kidney varieties which were regarded as civilian arms. The long, slender blades were considered an effective means of dealing at close range with plate armour. The distinctive features of most common models (see pictures) were the designs of the guards and pommels.

Many frequently closely resemble, in miniature, contemporary swords because they were sometimes copied from them. Furthermore, swords and quillon daggers were sometimes made as matching pairs. Many other patterns are thought to resemble swords purely because of their unmistakable cross guards. This was predomi-

nantly a military weapon with slender, narrow, double-edged, slightly diamond section blade with raised central rib. The cruciform guards made up a straight middle section terminating in straight or very slightly forward-curving quillons. These were often tipped with circular or lozenge-shaped knobs. Hilts were rather long in relation to the overall weapon length. Pommels were often of miniature wheel shape some of which had raised, round central bosses. Other pommels matched in a rather delicate way, the slender curving quillons of the guard, but these were set upon the tang curving upwards (see picture). Later patterns of this dagger will be studied in Chapter IV.

Rondel Daggers: first half 14th – late 16th centuries

This arm was mainly a military one frequently used by the armoured knight. Their appearance is very distinctive due to the pronounced roundels, or discs, sited at right angles to the grip, thus forming circular, octagonal, or hexagonal guards and matching pommels. To simplify the categorisation of this diverse dagger group, consider any which have matching guards and pommels as being a Rondel. The weapon became extensively popular, being used in much of western and northern Europe. They have straight, slender, tapering blades which can be either single- or double-edged, and slightly triangular shaped. Single-edged ones were often hollow ground. These were ideal for stabbing strokes and achieving narrow and deep

penetrating wounds through chinks in armour. They vary considerably in quality and manner of constructions (see pictures). Pommels and guards were often made from two joined convex plates, whilst some were more elaborate, comprising composite and rather complex layers of various materials such as bone, horn and wood. Some guards/pommels consist of only single plates. Grips appear in many forms; some have spiral or horizontal bindings, cheaper varieties just a simple wooden tube. Others are much grander incorporating carved horn with gilt-bronze mounts. The grips of later examples were frequently retained by a distinctive series of large, hollow, tubular brass rivets.

Quillon daggers were predominantly employed as a military weapon; note forward curving quillon and marked similarity with contemporary swords. Example is possibly English of the late 14th C.
THE BOARD OF TRUSTEES OF THE ROYAL ARMOURIES. (NEG NO: A3/696)

Baselards.
Note similar construction of these four very popular daggers. They have classic H shaped pommels and hilt form whilst the second from the left, about 1380, has an upside down guard style pommel.
THE BOARD OF TRUSTEES OF THE ROYAL ARMOURIES (NEG NO: A5661/8).

The Baselard: late 13th – late 15th centuries

As the name implies, this was originally designed in Switzerland but soon spread through central and western Europe becoming very popular. 'People from all walks of life carried baselards'[6]. It was predominantly a civilian arm used by all classes as the mandatory addition to normal costume, but by the early 14th century it was also carried by armoured knights as a second-line weapon in military operations. But 'in the fifteenth century, mounted knights generally ceased to carry the baselard and it became primarily the dagger of civilians and foot soldiers'[7]. It was made in a diversity of sizes. Each had a cross piece guard (which was really only a Quillon) matched by one on the pommel. These two sections formed a distinctive and easily recognised capital I, or an H on its side shape, in which the Quillons and pommel were often exactly matched (see pictures). Some blades were single-edged but the majority were double-edged. They had fullers (shallow grooves) stretching down from the guard for about one third of the blade length. The blades generally tapered evenly to the point. 'A few are single-edged, sometimes with a single narrow and shallow groove at the back'[8].

'Double-edged blades seem to have appeared very early also, however, and they are by far the more common among surviving examples'[9]. The hilt grip was of wood fixed to the tang with a large number of rivets. The Baselard was usually carried on the right side of the body or hung in front from the sword belt or girdle. It does not seem that they were suspended from a man's back.

Ballock or Kidney Daggers: late 13th – early 17th centuries

These developed during the late 13th century, probably in Flanders, and were predominantly a civilian arm but were also sometimes employed by soldiers. It was very popular, being widely used in northern Europe, particularly in England and the Low Countries. The form comprised a single-edged blade, similar to that of the knife dagger plus most distinctive guards resembling pronounced lobes, or kidneys (see picture), usually carved at the bottom section of the circular, phallus-shaped hilt. Sometimes, the lobes were carved individually and attached to the hilt riveted onto a metal guard plate. Hilts were round, swelling to a flattish, metal-capped top. One is depicted worn by an archer in the Luttrel Psalter (1370-1450). The Ballock knife was subsequently renamed; 'more prudish Victorian writers called it a kidney dagger'[10]. More details of this arm are given on pages 46 and 48.

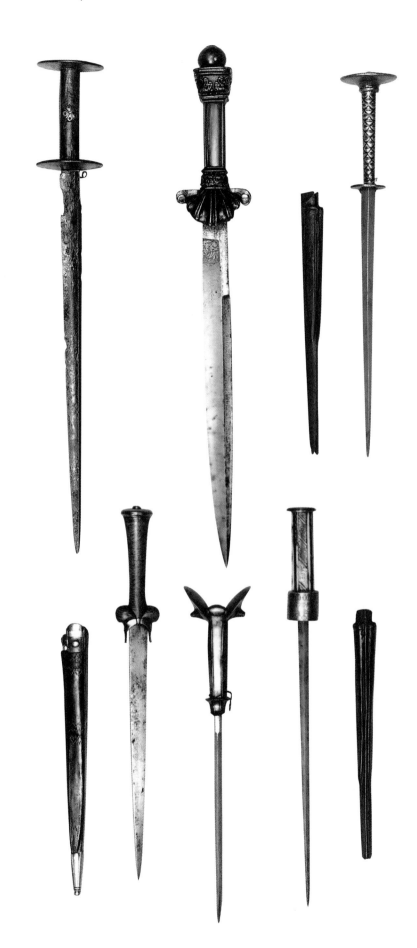

Various high quality 15th C French Daggers.

Top left: French Rondel of about 1440-1450, with its delicate form and decoration.

Top centre: French dagger of monumental form about 1500.

Top right: German Rondel of first half of 17th C with beautifully fashioned hilt and scabbard with pockets for two knives (missing).

Bottom left: high quality Flemish Kidney/Ballock dagger about 1450-1460 with scabbard.

Centre bottom: Italian (Venetian) Ear dagger of 16th C with two edged blade of diamond section.

Bottom right: German Rondel of about 1450 with sheath of wood bound with cuir bouilli; note restrained and neat hilt construction.

THE WALLACE COLLECTION
(PLATE NO: 138).

Ear Daggers: 16th century

We now briefly examine a curious weapon generally known as the Ear dagger on account of the two angled, sloping discs which make up the pommel area (see picture). They had no cross guard or more traditionally formed pommel. The 'ears' provided a snug and firm thumb position when the item was employed in very powerful over-shoulder strokes. The pattern became popular, for a time, in the 16th century. Blades were from about 8 to 10 inches long, usually double-edged, in diamond section with squared ricassos. It is considered that the 'pommel' formation of this dagger originates in the Middle East because of its similarity to Moorish and Turkish yataghans. The Wallace Collection has two very fine examples thought to derive from Venice and to have been made by Saracenic workmen. The weapon was also made in Spain. An exceptionally high quality example of this weapon is depicted in a picture of Edward VI, the son of King Henry VIII of England, in the National Gallery. (See plates 1 and 8, and page 28)

Notes

1   Howard L Blackmore, *Hunting Weapons*, Barrie & Jenkins, London
2, 3 A B Ward, 'Daggers', Museum of London catalogue
4, 6, 7, 8, 9 Harold L Peterson, *Daggers & Fighting Knives of the Western World*, Herbert Jenkins, London.
5, 10 Ewart Oakeshott, *European Weapons and Armour*, Lutterworth Press.

Hammer Headed dagger mid-to-late 15th C probably English. Iron hilt with hammer headed pommel with brass plate over prominent tang button, cusped quillon block and flattened horizontally recurved quillons widening towards both ends. Rectangular-sectioned tang widening slightly towards the blade. Straight, single-edged blade tapering to the spear point with flattened faces. Overall length: 16 inches; blade 12.25 inches.

THE BOARD OF TRUSTEES OF THE ROYAL ARMOURIES (NEG NO: A13/554).

Chapter IV

LATER MEDIEVAL AND 17TH CENTURY DAGGERS

We have so far examined daggers of the early Middle Ages and noted their evolution from the ubiquitous Scramasax, for centuries a most useful multi-purpose tool in northern Europe, with its perceptible Iron Age connotations, to the more delicately fashioned steel-bladed Ear dagger and high quality Rondels.

In this chapter, we shall see how many subsequent specimens frequently became even more finely formed, extravagantly embellished, and ornately decorated. Some are remarkable for being rather exaggerated in form and somewhat over-adorned, doubtless stemming from the ostentatious desire of wealthy patrons to impress their peers. This ambition was partly made possible by the continuously growing expertise and proficiency of sword- and dagger-smith master-craftsmen. The latter were assisted in the completion and enhancement of the finest weapons by the contribution of jewellers who specialised purely in expensive and exquisite weapon decoration. Doubtless, this trend reflected the growing wealth of European cities, in particular those of the Hanseatic League, and the civilising effects of the Renaissance, the influences of which must surely have contributed to the selection of classically elegant aesthetic designs and enriched hilt ornamentation.

Later Medieval Daggers

We continue our study of daggers into the late Middle Ages and thereafter progress to the middle of the 18th century. Throughout much of this period daggers remained a common and popular male accoutrement. The aristocracy regarded it now almost exclusively as a dress and status symbol. The mass of the population, however, still considered it a most useful multi-purpose tool and means of self-defence.

Later Quillon and Left Hand Daggers

We appreciate that the Quillon dagger, from about 1180 to 1450, was primarily a military weapon. 'During the 16th century the quillon dagger continued to be popular, although the hilt no longer resembled that of the contemporary sword'[1]. This was because sword hilts had developed into more intricate forms. About 1500, some Quillon patterns changed due to their new association with the practice of duelling. They were used in conjunction with the rapier to provide the swordsman with an additional defensive and offensive arm. They incorporated a forward ring to furnish additional protection to the left-hand thumb. It is pertinent now briefly to examine the rapier because of its direct influence on the design of some daggers and their new combat role.

N European left-hand Quillon dagger of 1560. Plain iron hilt, the quillons curved towards blade and inclining to the outside with ring attached to the outside of the block. Oval section pommel tapers very gently to the tang button. Wooden grip is modern replacement. Blade has been cut down from a rapier and is straight and double edged from ricasso to point. A central fuller runs down each blade face for just over half its length with an engraved line decoration either side of it. Blade length: 11.25 inches, overall: 16³/₈ inches.

THE BOARD OF TRUSTEES OF THE ROYAL ARMOURIES. (NEG NO: A3/644).

Group of Left Hand Daggers.

On left: German dagger of 1600 with steel hilt originally blued, consisting of pommel, straight quillons, oblong central block and small side ring. Slender sharply tapering blade of square section with deep central groove pierced with tiny circular holes. Blade: 11.5 inches, overall: 15.75 inches.

On right: Italian dagger of 1600. Bright steel hilt consisting of pommel, short straight quillons and oval side ring. Wood grip spirally ribbed and bound with copper wire. Heavy wavy blade with reinforced point and deep central groove pierced with series of holes. Blade: 10.6 inches, overall: 16 inches.

Second from right: German/Saxon dagger of 1590. Steel hilt consisting of pommel with prominent button, arched quillons and side ring. Elements of guard are decorated with V section fluting. Wooden grip bound with copper and steel wires. Diamond section blade with central ridge flanked by two pairs of narrow grooves. The blade narrows then swells near the point. Blade: 10.6 inches, overall: 15.6 inches.

Second from left: Geman dagger of 1600. Steel hilt now corroded to a hard black patina comprising fluted pommel, straight quillons springing from central block and thick side ring. Straight saw edge blade with prominent medial ridge on each side, the ridge is bordered by narrow double grooves pierced with groups of small holes. Blade: 10.8 inches, overall: 15.5 inches.

THE BOARD OF TRUSTEES OF THE ROYAL ARMOURIES (NEG NO: A8/221).

The Rapier and Left-Hand Daggers

Rapiers originated in France and Spain about the mid 16th century, and their popularity rapidly spread across Europe. This symbolised a more flamboyant and elegant age, albeit one of obvious contradictions – elegant manners and dirty lace, the poems of Milton and public executions. The weapon comprised a long, narrow, highly tempered, double-edged blade with a hilt initially of closely set curving bars (swept hilt). This provided essential hand protection as men rarely now wore the medieval mailed or plate gauntlet. As time passed, hilts gradually became smaller, whilst blades were shortened. Most blades were produced in specialist centres such as Toledo and Valencia in Spain, Solingen and Passau in Germany, and Milan and Brescia in Italy. Rapiers were predominantly the arm of civilians designed to be held in one hand whilst making well-aimed thrusts at an adversary from some distance. Duelling codes and methods of fighting were formulated. Gentlemen attended fencing schools to learn, then practise, sword-fighting techniques. 'It was the privilege of all gentlemen from a duke downwards, to wear swords and to murder one another by rule'[2].

About 1630 it was realised that additional offensive protection would be an advantage; the left-hand Quillon dagger was invented. It was called by various names: left-hand, main-gauche and just Quillon daggers. Their purpose was to catch or deflect an opponent's sword blade and, if the opportunity arose, to kill an adversary with a straight thrust or overarm stab. The blades of these are most usually double-edged and robust enough to withstand a blow from a sword/swept hilt rapier without snapping. Sometimes, dagger blades were perforated with small holes to reduce weight and thus combat fatigue (see picture). Important Quillon dagger modifications were: the top blade section (below the hilt) was flattened and the edges blunted to accommodate the finger and thumb enabling the dagger to be more accurately directed onto a target; and to protect these a side ring was sited at the centre of the cross guard to protect the thumb. Both blade sides often had a high central rib to increase the blade strength. Dagger pommels were remarkable for their differing shapes but most were elaborate. Guards usually curved forward towards the blade (see picture) to hold or deflect a hostile thrust. A most ingenious and sophisticated defensive dagger was the triple-bladed one. This incorporated three blades, two of which were activated by a spring control button which caused the two side blades to spring out. They were most effective in trapping and holding an opponent's rapier or dagger. (See pictures: plate 2 bottom.)

Duelling with swords reached its peak of popularity about 1770. Thereafter duels were fought with flint-lock duelling pistols, a less fatiguing means of settling differences. Gradually, the need for personal protection declined whilst social attitudes towards duelling became more hostile. The practice eventually ceased about 1820.

(This page)

Quillon Daggers

Left: Scots or English Quillon dagger 1608. Associated side ring and spatulate quillons chiselled with floral patterns. Hollow ground, diamond section blade with short ricasso etched on one face. The two blade faces are inlaid in copper with a mark; the blade etched with decorative patterns and on two faces with partially obscured inscription. Traces of gilding remain in etching. Blade: 10.4 inches, overall: 14.7 inches.

Centre: Quillon dagger 1636. Blade of Dudgeon type with thick blade sharpened for three inches from the point. Both faces coarsely engraved with floral patterns, on one side the date 1636 and on the other the maker's mark. On back is engraved; 'Pro Aris Et Focis' (For faith and home). Blade: 9.3 inches, overall: 13.8 inches.

Right: North European Quillon dagger. Hilt late 17th C, blade of 18th C. Iron hilt with rounded pommel with slight dip around tang button, arched lobate quillons flattened in the plane of blade springing from small ecusson. Iron hilt with silver patterns of classical busts of a young hero and foliage. Short blade of hollow triangular section is from an 18th C small sword. Blade: 8.25 inches, overall: 13.5 inches.

THE BOARD OF TRUSTEES OF THE ROYAL ARMOURIES (NEG NO: 48/965)

(Opposite page)

High quality Quillon daggers 16th to 17th C

Top row from left:
A Italian left-hand dagger with sheath about 1600. Spherically fluted pommel and diagonally fluted wire bound grip, straight quillons of flattened section widening towards ends and single side ring. Hilt encrusted in silver. Sharply ridged blade of diamond section at point with four pierced grooves. Sheath of wood bound with green velvet. Blade: 10³/₁₆ inches.
B Italian left-hand dagger about 1600 with flattened cylindrical pommel, fluted wire-bound grip, curved quillons of flattened oval section widening at the ends and single side ring. Blade of pronounced diamond section at the point and with six pierced grooves. Ricasso flattened on inner side for the thumb. Blade: 11³/₁₆ inches.
C Italian (?) left-hand dagger about 1600 with oviform pommel, fluted silver and steel wire bound grip, curved quillons of oval section widening towards ends, single side ring, hilt decorated with marks, scrolls and rosettes encrusted in silver on blackened ground; sharply ridged blade of diamond section at the point and with six pierced grooves. Blade: 11³/₈ inches.

Bottom row from left:
D A rather unusual 17th C quillon dagger with English blade (1610) with hilt which does not belong to it, being out of character. Fluted spherical pommel, curved quillons also fluted and swelling at the ends. Spirally fluted grip bound with copper wire. Diamond section blade with each face slightly hollowed. Blade: 9⁵/₈ inches. The group of daggers to which this belongs have proved to be of later date and more numerous than was previously believed. Collectors are recommended to read full details of all these daggers in the Wallace Collection Arms Catalogue, Volume II, starting with study of plate number 141.

A B C

D E F G

E Italian (?) left-hand dagger about 1600. Cylindrical pommel chiselled with frieze of mounted warriors, wire bound grip spirally fluted, short straight quillons of circular section swelling at the ends; single decorated side ring. Blade of flat diamond section with central groove deeply cut and pierced. Overall length: 14$^7/_8$ inches.

F Italian left-hand dagger of 1610. Small oviform pommel of ten facets, restored wire bound grip, straight quillons of flattened hexagonal section widening towards the ends, single side ring. Metal parts of the hilt are inlaid with gold arabesques of great delicacy: sharply ridged blade diamond section at point with four pierced grooves. Blade: 7$^1/_{12}$ inches.

G Italian left-hand dagger and sheath, about 1590. Hollow flattened cylindrical pommel pierced and chiselled with strap work loops enclosing small equestrian figures; diagonally fluted wire bound grip, curved quillons pierced and chased with recumbent figures terminating in pierced discs containing busts. Single side ring decorated like quillons. Diamond section blade the ricasso stamped on both sides with maker's mark. Sheath of wood bound in tooled leather. Blade: 9$^3/_{16}$ inches.

All items at THE WALLACE COLLECTION.

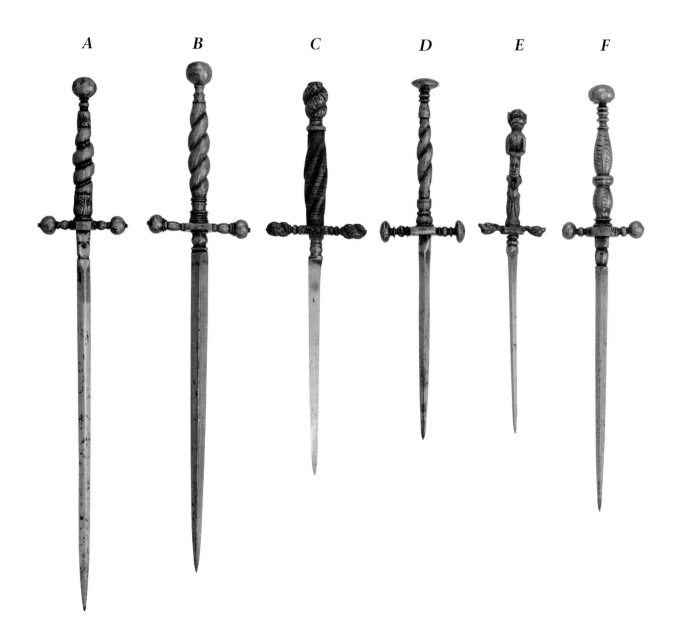

A   B   C   D   E   F

Italian Stilettos
From left to right:
A & B, late 16th C.
C, 16th C.
D, Multi-purpose Gunner's stiletto 16th C. One blade face side was a graduated scale, now illegible, apart from the zeroes used to calculate the weight of round shot for a given calibre of gun.
E, 16th or 17th C.
F, late 16th C.
THE BOARD OF TRUSTEES OF THE ROYAL ARMOURIES. (NEG NO: A8/224)

Traditional Stilettos 16th-17th centuries

The Stiletto is a weapon with considerable, perhaps over-exaggerated reputation for employment in murky deeds. It was introduced during the late 16th century but became more widespread in the 17th century. It first originated in Italy, particularly in the north. It was usually a rather small, or even tiny weapon with steel chiselled hilts intended for stabbing. The author, who has seen many different examples, was surprised to find that some are so very diminutive. Maybe this feature made them easier to conceal and, perhaps, because

some ladies may have possessed the dinky patterns. Interesting research of sixteen examples in The Wallace Collection revealed: five German, ten Italian and one of uncertain provenance. German models made between 1600 and 1615 had blade lengths ranging from 13.75 to 16.25 inches approximately. Italian examples, of which six were Brescian, fashioned between 1615 and 1660, possessed much shorter blades ranging from 6.25 to 13.25 inches. But, the majority of these were under 8 inches. The one of uncertain provenance has a blade of 14.25 inches, indicating Germany as the likely area of manufacture.

Blades are usually rectangular or triangular in shape with very narrow points; quillons were often tipped with knobs. A popular pattern was made from one complete piece of steel indicating high standards of steel cutting. Pommels vary considerably in form and are found in ovi-form, cone, barrel, spherical, pear and acorn shapes. Some are fashioned in a most detailed manner incorporating artistically wrought animals or human features. Although most were extensively used from about 1600 to 1660, Stilettos continued in fairly extensive use until about 1750. Indeed, they may possibly still be used today in modified forms. (See page 43 for details of Gunner's Stilettos)

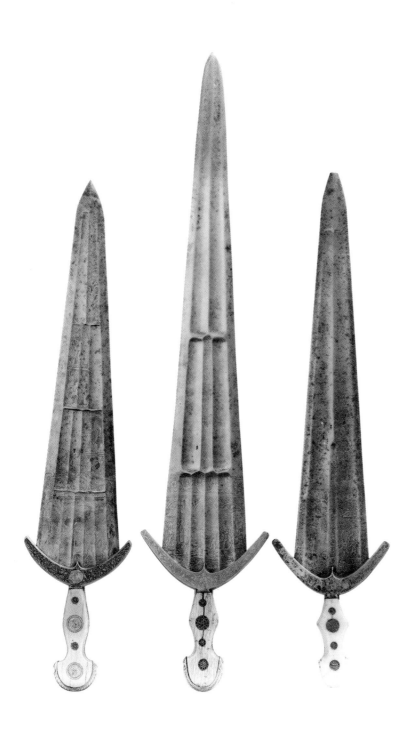

Cinquedas
A group of high quality Cinquedas at The Wallace Collection.

Left *Italian (Ferrarese) dagger about 1500. acc no: 746. Arch shaped ivory hilt, mounted with gilt bronze decorated with pair of lyre shaped acanthus leaves in low relief. Ivory plaques in pommel and grip inlaid with coins. Blade of flat diamond section with hollowed sunk panels and heavily decorated. Blade: 19 1/8 inches.*

Centre *Italian (Venetian) about 1490. acc no: 745. This is obviously a sword on account of its large size. Arched hilt shod in bronze gilt, decorated with profile bust and nude female figures in low relief. Grip and pommel are faced with ivory plaques inlaid on both sides with four, circular filigree ornaments in brass steel quillons of oblong flattened section sharply forward curved. Blade of flat diamond section with hollowed panels from hilt to point. Both sides with etched decorations. Inscription up the narrow panel. Blade: 25 7/8 inches.*

Right *Italian (Venetian) about 1470. acc no: 741. Markedly curved quillons; grip faced with thick ivory plaques inlaid with four circular filigree brass ornaments. Blade of flattened diamond section, with two shallow grooves decorated with allegorical subjects of winged horses and amorini etched in gilt. About half an inch is missing. Blade 20 1/8 inches.*

THE WALLACE COLLECTION

Cinquedas 1470-1560

This weapon is remarkable for its immediately recognisable form, the richness of its decoration, and the difficulty in deciding if examples are daggers or swords (see pictures). It was a civilian arm used predominantly in Italy from about 1480 to 1560. 'It was carried across the buttocks as shewn in a painting of the Crucifixion by Boccacino. The name arises from the five fingers' breadth of the blade.'[3] The production and carriage of Cinquedas was generally confined to Italy. Some have marked similarities to ancient classical swords. A fascinating study of the fourteen examples in The Wallace Collection revealed: four have blades over 20 inches which can be regarded as swords; the five with blades between 13 and 20 inches are presumably sword daggers; whilst the remaining five have blades under 13 inches and can be assumed to be true daggers. Early patterns have substantial sword-like, triangular blades some 5 inches wide just below the guard. These were markedly larger and longer than the later types. This most general trend is confirmed by specimens in The Wallace Collection where Cinquedas made between 1470 and 1500 were much larger (the biggest blade, made in 1490, is just under 26 inches long) than those fashioned between 1530 and 1560. However a few daggers were also made with very short blades of only 5-6 inches.

The common feature of most Cinquedas was the rich, copious, highly artistic and classic imaginativeness of their decoration. This strongly indicates the sophisticated artistry of Italian craftsmen. Diverse forms and types of decoration were applied to the hilts and blades, including engraving, etching, gilding, blueing and damascening. It is the luxurious and extravagant embellishing of these weapons which causes them, like the Landsknecht daggers (see below) to become the target of 19th-century (and 20th-century?) counterfeiters. Collectors should take the very greatest care before acquiring one of these items and demand authenticated provenance details before purchasing.

Landsknecht Daggers 1550-1640

This dagger possibly developed from the Baselard which, as we know, originated in Switzerland in the late 13th century. The new weapon was used from about 1550 to 1630. It was made in Germany, particularly in the south, and in Switzerland. They are immediately recognisable by their metal scabbards with bulbous chape and central sections all of which are heavily decorated, and noticeable hilts (see pictures). The form of the pommels was often of rosette, pear, or spherical shape. Some just had neat flat tops. Grips were usually of conical form tapering to the guard. The latter were made of blackened or russeted steel often silver plated and enhanced with niello, or blued steel. Sometimes wooden hilts were wire- or leather-bound. Guards were either simple straight cross ones, or of trefoil-shaped downward-facing quillons. Because of the extensive decoration of this arm they were often counterfeited. The author recently saw a magnificent counterfeit example which he was compelled to admire because of the very high craftsmanship standards which had been devoted to its creation. Collectors are therefore warned to take particular care before purchasing one of these.

Such daggers were used by Landsknecht soldiers who belonged to the famous (infamous?) corps of infantry mercenaries hired by the Emperor Maximilian. This large unit was formed about 1492. The soldiers, frequently represented in old manuscripts, were most distinctive by virtue of their arms and costumes. They often discarded metal helmets to wear instead broad-brimmed hats adorned with ostrich feathers. They carried pikes or halberds, swords with noticeable S-shaped, or two ringed quillons and the characteristic daggers.

**Landsknecht Dagger
& Sheath**
German about 1550.
THE WALLACE COLLECTION.
ACC NO: A752.

Hauswehre Daggers 1400-17th century

This widely used arm, the title of which means 'home arm' or 'home weapon', embraces several types of multi-purpose implements in the form of short heavy swords, hangers, and daggers. These originated in Switzerland. They vary considerably in length and size and so many could be used in a variety of artisan and farming tasks as well as for defence. The larger ones had robust and rather crude single-edged blades, parallel for most of their length, with pronounced blade backs with blade edges tapering slightly to the point.

Simple, generally straight cross guards were sometimes fitted. Grips comprised strips of bone, or wood, attached to the broad tang. It has been suggested that this weapon originated from the Scramasax dagger to which it bears a resemblance, and because the latter was widely used in northern Germany, from the 7th to the 10th century. A few had pommels, but most were topped with just a button. The Museum of London has a most interesting small Hauswehre dagger.

Holbein Daggers 1540-1600

Holbein Dagger
Hilt of dark wood and quillons of boat shape form; diamond section blade of 9$^1/_8$ inches. Sheath of wood covered with gilt bronze depicting scene from legend of William Tell. This example is actually a 19th C copy but is a very accurate representative example of the type of 1575-85.
THE WALLACE COLLECTION ACC NO. A770

This dagger is called 'Holbein' because many of the weapons' sheaths are ornately decorated with a design based on a picture by the artist Hans Holbein the Younger for use upon a dagger sheath. The original picture is retained in the Basel Museum. The drawing was called 'The Dance of Death'. The dagger is of Swiss origin with original form based upon the Hausewehre dagger which we examined above. Hilts are dis-

tinctively shaped like cuttlefish bones. Blades were rather wide, double-edged, leaf-shaped and of diamond section. It appears that the arm was produced in two categories: as a highly decorated, expensively fashioned pattern with sheaths enhanced with gilt copper or gilt bronze for members of the upper class; and a much plainer, utilitarian one used by the lower classes.

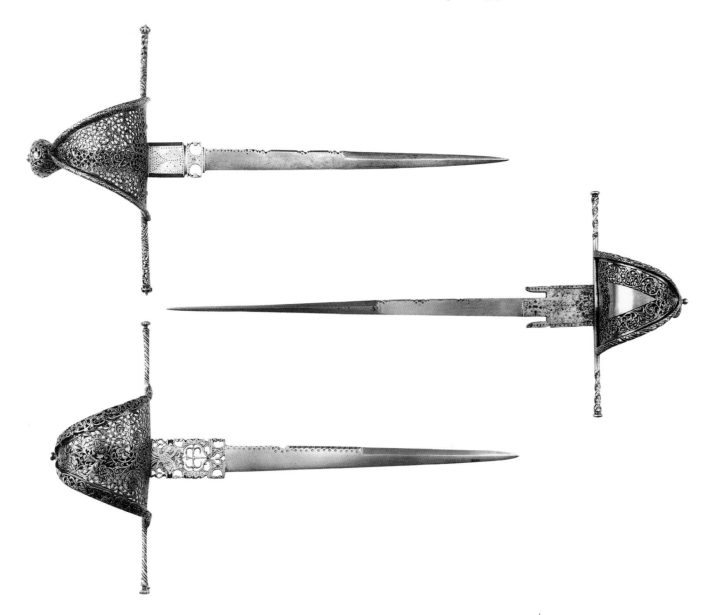

Spanish high quality left-hand daggers from The Wallace Collection.

Bottom. acc No: A830. Spanish left-hand dagger about 1650. Spherical pommel spirally fluted with button; leather bound grip, straight quillons, spirally fluted ending in rosette-shaped knobs. Large triangular knuckle guard, the end strongly recurved, pierced and chased with scrolls of flowers and foliage. Triangular section blade, with back edge knotched and decorated with small circles, changing to flattened diamond section towards point. Flat, wide ricasso pierced with holes for sword breaking and an oval depression, on reverse side of ricasso for thumb. Length: 16³/₄ inches.

Centre. acc No: A834. Spanish or Italian left-hand dagger about 1650. Straight quillons spirally fluted at ends and tipped with flat buttons. Triangular knuckle guard with solid, diagonally fluted edge with broad bands of foliage in scroll form pierced and broadly chiselled surrounding a plain triangle in centre. Triangular section blade changing to diamond section towards point; back edge notched and diagonally serrated. Broad, flat ricasso decorated with circles. Two projections for sword breaking with serrated edges. Reverse ricasso side has deep depression for thumb. Length: 19.5 inches.

Top. acc No: 827. Spanish left-hand dagger about 1630-50. Pronounced pear shaped pommel pierced and chased with foliage. Hollow steel grip of circular section; straight quillons finished with knobs triangular knuckle bow the edges turned over with two small shells on inner side. The guard is elaborately pierced and chiselled on both sides with scrolled foliage. Blade of triangular section at hilt, the back edge knotted diagonally, changing to diamond section at point. Flat ricasso has two holes for sword breaking and usual depression for thumb. Length 16⁷/₁₆ inches. THE WALLACE COLLECTION.

Spanish Left-Hand Daggers 1625-1730

This left-hand arm is given separate paragraph mention for three reasons; firstly because of its exceptionally high design and manufacturing standards; secondly, because its use continued into the 18th century long after left-hand dagger usage declined in most of central and northern Europe, and finally because its attractive form epitomises the highest dagger manufacturing standards. These features excite the imagination of dagger collectors (see picture on page 41). It was introduced in Spain early in the 17th century and used there and throughout the Spanish empire. The dagger is immediately recognisable having a blade of triangular section at the hilt stretching down to diamond section at the point. The broad ricasso often has a marked depression area for the thumb on the inner side. The blade back edge is often fitted with circular holes or projecting forward sections for sword blade breaking. The most distinctive section is the very broad, curved knuckle bow which is usually in triangular shape but also, sometimes, in rounded form. The quillons are at once noticeable being long, spirally fluted, narrow, and straight.

The area of finest decoration is the knuckle bow. Some later models were rather plain but the majority of earlier examples were decorated in an exceptionally skilled manner. The recurved edges are often scrolled, whilst the centre is etched, pierced, and chiselled in a highly skilful artistic way to produce fine and beautiful patterns representing, for example, flowers, birds, animals, and leaves. For duelling they were a most efficient form of left-hand dagger. It could be suggested, with considerable justification, that for collectors this arm represents the epitome of any dagger collection. They are of fascinating and beautiful construction. But their authenticity should be carefully checked before buying to ensure the item is definitely genuine. It is recommended that, before buying, arrangements be made for the example to be examined by an expert. The Wallace Collection, in Manchester Square in London, has a magnificent collection of this dagger form.

Notes

1 Frederick Wilkinson, *Edged Weapons*, Guinness Signatures, London
2 H O Arnold-Foster, *A History of England*, Cassell
3 Sir James Mann KCVO, FBA, HON. VPSA

Chapter V

DUAL-PURPOSE AND EASTERN DAGGERS

During the first half of the 17th century, some fascinating daggers were fashioned in a particularly novel and ingenious manner. Their aim was to provide, within one arm, gadgets which could undertake other useful services in addition to that of a close quarter weapon. These items are rare and all remarkable for the highest steel cutting production standards. They were also often highly embellished and decorated in a most attractive and artistic manner. The common example was a left-hand dagger which could be converted into a three bladed one by pressing a button causing two side blades to spring out. (See plate 2)

Many others were produced to assist gunnery artillery units which, by this time, had become fairly technical and employed mathematical calculations. A well-known one was the Artillery, or Gunner's Stiletto, used for a variety of tasks. One pattern incorporated two blades, each of triangular section, forming a single blade of diamond section when closed together. The open blades thus provided a pair of dividers (or compass) used to determine accurately distances on a map. Some blades were calibrated with numbers, enabling the dagger to be used to calculate the calibre of cannon barrel bores and the diameter of cannon balls to ensure correctly sized balls were employed in the right gun. The Gunner's Stiletto could also be used to open the cartridge of the explosive charge before firing, after this had firstly been inserted within the barrel. It was also used to clean out the gun touch hole to ensure the correct quantity of the priming gunpowder charge rapidly reached down to the main explosive charge.

Some models were equipped with other multi-use gadgets. A most unusual arm in The Wallace Collection confirms this practice. It is a three-purpose German Stiletto, of about 1660, designed as a dagger, powder flask/primer, and spanner. The dagger grip is hollow, providing a priming powder receptacle. From this main supply source one correctly measured powder charge can pass to the frontal pommel cavity and thence, when appropriate, to a wheel-lock pistol. The final gadget is incorporated on quillons of rounded section cut square on the inner sides at the ends to provide a spanner for the wheel-lock firearm. (See picture on page 44.)

The Sword Breaker

A few left-hand daggers were produced primarily as sword blade breakers. They possessed most complicated blades, comprising one conventional blade cutting edge, and another fashioned with numerous deep teeth, the edges bevelled but connected to a spring catch. This arrangement allowed the sword blade to be caught within the teeth where it was locked in by the activation of the spring catch. The blade could then be easily snapped by a sharp turn of the left wrist. (See plate 2, top row.)

*Gunner's Stiletto combined
with primer and sheath.
Probably German, about
1660. Overall length:
14 1/2 inches.*
THE WALLACE COLLECTION.
ACC NO: 1309.

Eastern Daggers

Readers are recommended to study Plate 8 to clarify more easily this complex subject.

For many years, European collectors in general applied the label 'Oriental' to virtually every area outside Europe and America, and usually in a slightly derogatory tone. This lack of perception is in the process of being redressed, and the finest quality Eastern weapons are increasingly sought after. Some can command very high prices. Even so, Europe, and Western Europe particularly, still remains a veritable treasure house of 'Oriental' arms and armour since so much was brought back from areas in which colonial powers operated, especially in the 19th century. It is still, therefore, possible to find an assortment of such material at reasonable prices, whereas in their country of origin little remains on the market.

Royal and princely items are now too expensive for most collectors. However, utilitarian Eastern daggers, often more highly decorated and of better workmanship than their European counterparts, are not hard to find and represent excellent value. Eastern dagger collectors have always encountered identification and dating problems, and undoubtedly these will continue. The situation should change when more publications devoted to this subject are published. The interchange of culture, ideas, technologies, and decorative schemes, forms, and techniques throughout the East, and in Islamic nations particularly, have made dating and identification of their weapon products extremely difficult. The problem is aggravated because the designs and uses of weapons in the Middle East did not change much for several hundred years. So, the collecting of such items is a challenging pursuit. It is beyond the scope of this book to examine in detail the various forms and decoration of Eastern daggers. Those most often encountered come from the Indian sub-continent and the Middle East. They are often difficult to tell apart, so the term 'Indo-Persian' is used to classify them roughly. Weapons from the old Turkish Empire are still relatively com-

mon, and Far Eastern models, though less often seen, still exist in some quantity. The kris dagger from Indonesia and the Malay archipelago is perhaps the best known. In Japan, the sword is justly the most famous weapon, but the dagger is also very important and regarded as honourable because its manufacture involved the same skills as the sword. Daggers/knives from mainland Africa and the inner reaches of Asia, including China, are seldom encountered and so are not covered here.

'Indo-Persian' daggers are in four broad categories. These are: the Katar, the Jambiya, the Khanjar and the Kard or Pesh Kabz. A brief study of them may assist the collector.

The Indian 'Katar' is a thrusting weapon with transverse grip. It is the easiest to recognise. Some are 16th-century but most are 19th-century. Its style is purely Indian and rarely found outside that sub-continent. The 'Jambiya' was originally Arabian but can now be found in the Middle East and India. It generally has a sharply curved double-edged blade and assortment of hilt forms, the most common being a capital I shape. The 'Khanjar' of India and Persia is similar, but with less sharply curving blade. These periodically have a pistol grip hilt often carved from hardstone or jade.

The Kard or Pesh Kabz are acutely pointed daggers with straight or re-curved, single-edged blades. The Turks have their own versions of these, although the finest examples are usually of Persian origin. The most common Turkish dagger is the 'yataghan' with its distinctive 'eared' grip. Also popular throughout the Turkish Empire were the qama, or kindjal daggers, typical of which are the silver- and niello-mounted Cossack and Caucasian types. The latter has a straight double-edged blade shaped in a manner similar to the Roman *gladius* with a capital I hilt often fashioned in ivory or walrus tusk.

Chapter VI

DAGGERS OF SCOTLAND

Ballock Dagger & Sheath, Scottish or English c1620.

Left:
Hilt of wood of octagonal section swelling towards the top which terminates in a brass button. Two small, kidney-shaped swellings with concave steel washer immediately above the ricasso of the stiff, diamond section blade which is etched with foliate patterns, the date 1620, and a mark. Black leather sheath with tooled decoration. Overall length: 15.4 inches, blade: 11.4 inches.
Traditionally the dagger of Colonel Blood (1618-1680) who stole the Crown Jewels in 1671.

Right:
Similar to arm on the left of the picture but smaller, undated, and etched with a different mark. Traditionally the dagger of Colonel Blood's accomplice in his theft of the Crown Jewels. Overall length: 12.1 inches, blade: 9.2 inches.

THE BOARD OF TRUSTEES OF THE ROYAL ARMOURIES. (NEG NO: A5759/1)

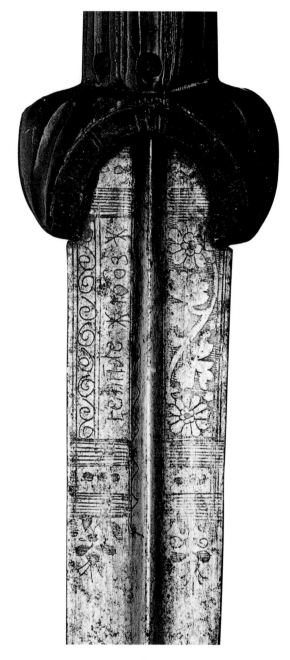

Above:
Dudgeon Dagger, British
(Scottish) c1603.
THE BOARD OF TRUSTEES OF
THE ROYAL ARMOURIES.
(NEG NO: A16/577)

Left:
The same Dudgeon Dagger
as above depicted with its
sheath of tooled leather.
THE BOARD OF TRUSTEES OF
THE ROYAL ARMOURIES.
(NEG NO: A16/572)

The Dudgeon Dagger 1580-1650

This weapon stemmed from the Ballock/Kidney dagger so widely used in Britain and Flanders from the late 13th to the second half of the 16th century, and which we studied in Chapter III. During the early 16th century the very obvious sexual connotations of this arm, so deliberately presented, gradually became more restrained until the weapon was succeeded by a different dagger in the mid-16th century. This was the rather fearsome Dudgeon dagger which did, to a limited degree, retain one of its predecessor's characteristics – small bulbous lobes at the hilt base. The new arm was produced in both Scotland and England. Dudgeons had straight, or slightly tapered hilts, in hexagonal, octagonal or round form. One interesting feature is that hard wood seems to have been most commonly used in the hilt, fashioned in ebony, rootwood, briar, heather root, or holly wood. The slightly rounded pommel top was capped with a brass button concealing the end of the tang. At the hilt base the curved wood lobes were fronted by an inserted, curved, metal, protective guard plate. This was retained to the lobes with pins. Blades of between 10 and about 13 inches long were of single- or double-edged form tapering slightly on both edges to form a long point. Some were of diamond section, others were of flat form with substantial blade backs. These rather resemble Highland dirk blades (see next section). A few had pronounced central, raised blade dividers. Sometimes, blades were fairly skilfully decorated with inlaid engraving (see picture). The overall length of Dudgeons ranged from about 12 to 16 inches. They were carried in a leather scabbard.

The Highland Dirk 1550-Today

Before describing the next weapon, we should perhaps consider the country in which it was so widely employed as an offensive arm. This was at a time when civilian dagger carriage and use had markedly declined in the rest of Europe.

In 1700, the clan system still flourished in the Scottish Highlands, an area geographically isolated from the rest of Scotland. This fostered an insular attitude toward foreigners and some neighbours which was aggravated by centuries of hostility and feuding. Therefore, arms carriage and their efficient battle employment remained a prerequisite to clan survival. This was why everyday weapon use persisted far longer in the Highlands where, in 1685, some 200,000 armed men created a strikingly anomalous situation with the rest of Great Britain. The situation is well described in the book, *History of the Rebellion in the Year 1745* by John Hulme, who was a Jacobite prisoner. He stated that the Highlanders: 'always appeared like warriors; as if their arms had been limbs and members of their bodies, they were never seen without them; they travelled, they attended fairs and markets, nay went to church with their broadswords and dirks; and in later times with muskets and pistols'.

The commonest, popular weapon was the Dirk dagger and nearly every man carried one. Like other daggers, it was used for a variety of non military tasks and in game butchering, but its offensive fighting function was most important. Many blades were fashioned locally, but some were cut down from old two-handed broadswords, or broken one-handed basket-hilted broadswords. Dirks incorporating cut-down blades were potentially of much higher quality being of expensive steel imported from such countries as Germany and Italy. Many clansmen were very heavily armed, equipped with broadsword, dirk, shield (targe), pistols and a long arm. 'The weapons which they use are a longe basket hilt sworde, and a long kind of dagger broad in the back and sharp at ye pointe which they call a durke.'[1]

Weapons of the Highland Warrior.
An excellent portrayal of equipment carried by the well-armed clansman. Note the broadsword with its basket hilt extended to the rear providing extra wrist protection; the dirk with classic wedge-shaped blade stamped with maker's mark; the flint-lock operated Doune pistol; and bullet pouch, flint, powder horn and bullet mould pincers.
THE WEST HIGHLAND MUSEUM, FORT WILLIAM.

Four Highland Dirks of the late 17th and early 18th C.

The three splendid dirks on the left are of the late 17th C. Note their wedge-shaped blades, the straight hilt cut-off at the blade top, and highly ornate interlace hilt carving. These all belong to the second dirk-pattern group from which the standardised dirk of the early 18th C emerged.

The right hand dirk of the early 18th C, with its horn hilt and stylised lobes, possesses connotations with the Ballock and Dudgeon daggers and thus belongs to the first dirk group mentioned in the script.

TRUSTEES OF THE NATIONAL MUSEUMS OF SCOTLAND.

The Dirk originated from two sources and eventually merged into one uniform pattern. The first stemmed from the Dudgeon and Ballock dagger, hence its long pointed blade and small rounded lobes at the hilt base. The pommel had a flat top with sharply inward curved sides; the grip is circular with parallel sides terminating with the two lobes, which had become stylised in form, incorporating the curved, brass guard plate. The blade is long and wedge-shaped. The hilt decoration was generally meagre comprising groups of horizontal lines. Blade lengths were about 12 inches; overall lengths some 16 to 17 inches.

The second pattern also had a flat-topped pommel with sharply inward sloping sides at the top (like a soup plate). The wooden hilt is rather bulbous leading down to a wider section above the forte which terminates in a straight line across the blade. Initially, this model lacked a guard plate causing, not surprisingly, some dirks to lose parts of their hilts doubtless to an opponent's sword swing. Later models do incorporate a metal guard plate. The wooden hilts and pommels are generously and rather delightfully and beautifully carved in a series of Celtic and Viking Norse strap interlace patterns providing excellent hand grip (see pictures). Patterns incorporating such decoration are particularly emotive. Blade lengths were about 12-13 inches; overall lengths about 17-18 inches. The weapon was carried in a leather-bound wooden sheath on the outside of which was sometimes carried a small knife. Some dirks incorporated a saw on the back edge, similar to those on German hunting swords, used to butcher game.

Eventually, from about the early 18th century, the two design patterns merged. Subsequently their form incorporated, to some degree, characteristics of previous models. Pommels had slightly rounded tops but with less distinctive sides, hilts were slightly rounded and carved but in less distinctive and cultivated form than previously; lobes disappeared to be replaced by wider and more pronounced, slightly curved guard plates. Blades were similar to previous models, being generally broad-backed and single-edged. On some, the blades were double-edged at the bottom section only. The previous saw backs were replaced in simulated manner with wavy decoration. Subsequently, dirk design was influenced more by adornment considerations than combat priorities. Hilts became baluster-shaped, eventually culminating in pronounced thistle form.

Decoration rapidly became over-excessive due to the profusion of engraved silver, or German silver work, widespread adoption of Cairngorms or other stones, and utilisation of round-headed, white metal pins sited in pattern forms. Such examples were more appropriate for wear at Caledonian balls than for use on the battlefield. Soldiers in Highland regiments, however, continued to carry the more utilitarian patterns for combat duty. In the Bayonet section of this book we shall examine the high combat effectiveness of the dirk. It is, however, stressed that, although carried in the left hand, it was NOT a main gauche weapon because protection was afforded by the shield. Its use was primarily offensive. In battle, it was wielded offensively in conjunction with the broad sword periodically enabling clansmen to kill two opponents almost simultaneously one with each weapon. The main occasion upon which it was used for defence was when an opponent managed to get under the warrior's long basket hilted sword blade preventing that weapon being effective at such very close quarters. The dirk, held in the left hand, was then used in an upward thrust stroke to dispatch such an assailant. Highlanders carried an additional small knife called the black knife (*skean-dhu*). This is a single-edged knife mounted with a black bog oak hilt carried under the arm in concealed manner or, later, in the stocking top. The strong blade, some 3.5 to 4.5 inches long, resembles a miniature version of the dirk blade. The wooden hilt is flat except at the top where it leans forward. The front face was carved in a similar manner to the dirk. Collectors interested in acquiring dirks should ensure that they purchase, if possible, a rather plain and simple one, which is pre-1745 and thus more likely to have Jacobite connotations.

Notes

1. An account of Shetland, Orkney and the Highlands of Scotland, written by Richard James (1592-1638). *Orkney Record and Antiquary Society*, Vol 1, 1953. Quoted by Dunbar, op. cit. p201.
General Reference: John Wallace, *Scottish Swords and Dirks*, Stackpole Books.

Chapter VII

DAGGER STATUS AND REPUTATION

Status

We have studied the evolution and development of the dagger from early times to the mid-18th century. During this long period it fulfilled most useful functions. Its role as a multi-purpose tool enabled it to be used as a defensive or offensive weapon, an eating utensil, and an implement for performing diverse household and farming tasks. It was also a mandatory dress item and frequently a status symbol. These were the most common dagger functions for many centuries. It was a very popular and most versatile implement. Some patterns, such as the Quillon and many Rondels were specifically military weapons whilst others, like the Baselard and single-bladed knife dagger, were used by civilians. This general custom did not prevent other dagger forms being carried by soldiers or civilians. Its display by so many was also prompted by custom and as an ostentatious means of denoting status and wealth. We noted how, from the early 16th century onwards, several very different and much more finely fashioned and richly decorated daggers were introduced across Europe. This trend subsequently continued with the emergence of even finer and more ornate arms such as the highly sophisticated Cinqueda and costly Holbein daggers. To a degree, perhaps, the carriage of such fine and elaborate weapons was dictated more by fashion and the wish to present a splendid appearance than for martial or utilitarian purposes. This trend became more marked as the centuries progressed.

Dagger significance declined for a variety of reasons. The invention of the bayonet, which we study in Part II, during the second half of the 17th century, caused a marked dwindling of dagger carriage by soldiers. The waning custom of using the left-hand dagger with the rapier, in the second half of the 17th century, reduced its fighting purpose. Dagger value in undertaking a multiplicity of household and farming chores, for centuries their predominant secondary purpose, was diminished by the gradual introduction of new, specialist artisan tools and the emergence of forks for eating. To some degree dagger decline was also synonymous with that of swords and edged weapons generally. 'The duel in the 17th century had been fought at the push of the rapier; in the early 19th century, it was fought with pistols.'[1] Finally, it was the growing popular rejection of public arms wearing and the eventual cessation of duelling that caused dagger obsolescence with its use reduced to a few minor tasks. They retained some significance in one occupation at least. This was in hunting. A very large selection of instruments and weapons were used in this activity and often retained in a trouse. For example, for hunting there were: swords, sword-daggers, daggers, knives, hangers, dirks, and choppers. Some incorporated saw-backs for the butchering process. Full, very high quality kits of such instruments, including daggers, were produced (see picture page 53).

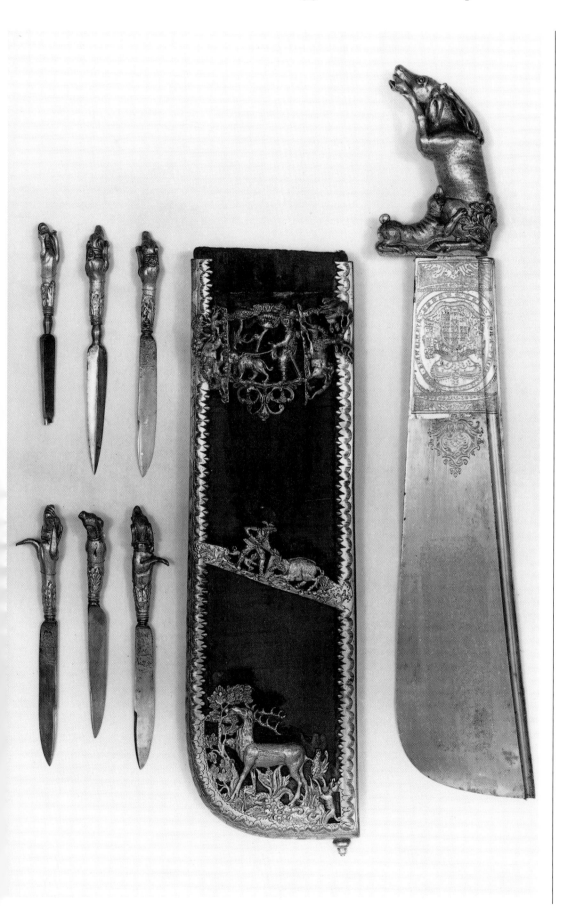

Set of Eviscerating Instruments, German, probably Solingen 1732.
A Waldpraxe or Trousse de Chasse consisting of a large knife, sheath and six small knives or implements. The knife with its handle of gilt bronze in the form of a stag attacked by a hound; the broad, heavy back-edged blade could be used as a knife and chopper. Overall length: 20 inches; blade: 14⅝ inches.
THE WALLACE COLLECTION

Reputation

'Is this a dagger which I see before me, the handle toward my hand?
Come, let me clutch thee: I have thee not, and yet I see thee still.'
Shakespeare, *Macbeth*, Act II, Scene I

We now all appreciate how the numerous advantages of the dagger caused its widespread use for many centuries. People strove within their financial limitations to acquire high quality, finely embellished examples. It is of the greatest interest that in the Middle Ages cheaper and cruder copies were often produced in significant numbers indicating the desire of many to emulate those possessing higher quality accoutrements.

Dagger reputation, however, was tainted by its periodic use, or alleged employment, in the commission of disreputable, secretive, and unsavoury deeds. Perhaps these are exaggerated; however, it became associated with assassinations performed without warning when the concealed weapon was suddenly flourished and used to kill. Consequently, it developed connotations with murky, cowardly assaults in dark alleys, upon shadowy staircases, and of hired murderers emerging from concealment behind an arras fatally to stab innocent, sleeping victims. So, its reputation was and still is somewhat tainted: how very different from that of the sword, wielded proudly in the open and regarded with awe and reverence as the symbol of knightly power and the instrument blessed by Christ for the suppression of the enemies of the true faith.

To a degree, some antipathy towards the dagger has remained unchanged up to modern times. This is, perhaps, partly due to the periodic, contemporary broadcasting of bloodthirsty films and television series depicting gangsters employing the stiletto. History is punctuated with accounts of daggers being used in assassinations and coup d'état attempts. On 15 March 44BC, Gaius Julius Caesar (100-44 BC), a very brave officer who disregarded the advice of the soothsayer!, was assassinated by a large group of conspirators including Cassius and Brutus who had planned the coup. They stabbed him repeatedly with their daggers. This took place in Rome in a room behind the theatre of Pompey which was being used for government business whilst the Senate was being rebuilt. In Anglo-Saxon times, the twenty-four-year-old King Edmund of England, who had served as a sixteen-year-old with King Athelstan at his famous victory at Brunanburg (937) was murdered. 'His promising reign, however, was cut brutally short in May 946 when, during the feast of St Augustine at Pucklechurch in Gloucester, he was stabbed to death by a criminal.'[2] The felon probably used a Scramasax dagger. A murder of particular brutality was that of Rizzio, secretary to Mary Queen of Scots, on 9 March 1566 at Holyrood Palace in Edinburgh. Whilst seated at supper with the Queen he was dragged away by several nobles and stabbed to death in an adjoining room. Perhaps the assassins used Dudgeon daggers. Lord Darnley held his wife to prevent her from intervening to save the victim.

To some degree the dagger regained, perhaps, a little social prestige during the rapier age when personal combat became less brutal. Its involvement in this highly formalised, more public display of dignified, regulated, martial endeavour, so preferable to the previous custom of murdering those with whom one disagreed at the hands of a band of armed retainers or clansmen, did something to restore its reputation.

We appreciate how daggers in Europe were carried by most men as a weapon, a useful tool, and a mandatory dress item for well over a thousand years. When its advantages and purpose eventually declined, and weapon carriage ceased, the arm was saved from complete obsolescence by its retention as a field sports gadget. 'In the nineteenth century, with the spread of so-called civilisation, the custom of wearing a general purpose knife practically ceased and the hunting knife became a specialised instrument.'[3]. However, its combat and military traditions were incorporated in the bayonet weapon which has continued in use until the present day.

Notes

1 G M Trevelyan OM, *English Social History*, Longman, Green and Co.
2 Robert Jackson, *Dark Age Britain*, Book Club Associates.
3 Howard L Blackmore, *Hunting Weapons*, Barrie & Jenkins, London.

Part II
THE BAYONET

Chapter I

THE EARLY BAYONET

The purpose of Part II of this book is to examine the evolution of the bayonet from its early origins to the present day. All major basic pattern changes throughout its history are studied and the reasons for their introduction explained. We shall see why it was such a particularly significant weapon for over 200 years. Finally, the reasons for the continued retention of the arm in regular army service today are analysed. The most important military significance of the arm occurred during the early stages of its use from about 1690 to 1720. In this period it caused far-reaching battlefield, weapon, and unit formation changes. These will be thoroughly investigated.

This part of the book is written for the following readers: those with general historical interests, students of military history, weapon collectors, wargamers, members of re-enactment societies, and military modellers. For the benefit of the latter, weapon pictures are supported by detailed captions including detailed specifications. Practical wargamers should also find information on battlefield bayonet usage of value when fighting their battles. Such data is particularly relevant to campaigns occurring between 1680 and 1815. Advice for collectors is regularly included throughout the script with emphasis particularly devoted to those who are about to begin a collection. For enthusiasts who have already accumulated several artefacts Part III is concerned with the preservation and conservation of such items. Many bayonet patterns are described, in words and pictures, with the aim of assisting collectors in achieving correct identification and classification of their own collection patterns.

Bayonet Origins

Bayonet origins are rather obscure due to myth, legend and the passage of time. We do know, however, that very early attempts were made to provide additional, personal protection for musketeers, and that the resulting arms employed could be regarded as the first type of bayonet. It should be explained that, in about 1580, only a few infantrymen were equipped with firearms. These used the arquebus, the charge of which was detonated by a smouldering match. By about 1600, the musket was introduced. This was more accurate, and could fire longer ranges than the arquebus. But it had disadvantages: 'it was so heavy that it had to be rested on a fork, and having a firing rate appreciably slower even than the forty rounds an hour of the arquebus'[1]. The musket detonation system was also caused by means of a smouldering match. Arquebusiers and musketeers were vulnerable to attack by enemy cavalry after they had discharged their firearms but before they could reload, despite being armed with swords. For this reason they were protected by pikemen units. But they really needed a more immediate form of personal defence.

Musket Rest 'Bayonet'

Exceptionally interesting and rare arm (acc No: 1330) in The Wallace Collection. This is a musket rest bayonet which has a concealed blade designed to provide additional protection to musketeers after they discharged their firearms. This experimental Italian weapon was made about 1600. Blade length: 28¹/₂ inches. THE WALLACE COLLECTION.

Some attempt, presumably on a trial basis, was made to overcome the periodic vulnerability of musketeers. It utilised the musket rest incorporated in which was an ingenious device comprising a long blade housed within the shaft. Surviving patterns are extremely rare but there is a splendid Italian one, of about 1600, in the Wallace Collection (acc No: A 1330). On this, a 28.5-inch-long blade of stiff, diamond shape is housed on the hollow rest shaft. This is released by giving the shaft a sharp forward jerk causing the blade to spring out of the head through an opening otherwise concealed by a hinged cover. It is then firmly held in the extended forward position by a spring-catch which engages in a slot in the neck. This provided a useful pike-type weapon when wielded with two hands.

Hunstman spearing a boar caught in a net. Note second huntsman announcing the success on his horn and robustness of boar spear. LE LIVRE DU ROY MODUS (1486).

Plate 1

Edward VI bearing a high quality Ear dagger

Plate 2

Top row, left to right:
Sword Breaker (1600),
German left-hand dagger (1620),
Italian left-hand dagger (1620),
Italian Dividers (1630-40)

Middle row:
German left-hand dagger and sheath (1615),
Italian Gunner's Stiletto (1650),
Italian left-hand dagger (1600),
German combined Stiletto, primer and sheath (1600),
French triple-bladed Plug Bayonet with scabbard (1660)

Bottom row:
German triple-bladed left-hand dagger (1600),
French triple-bladed left-hand dagger and sheath (1600)

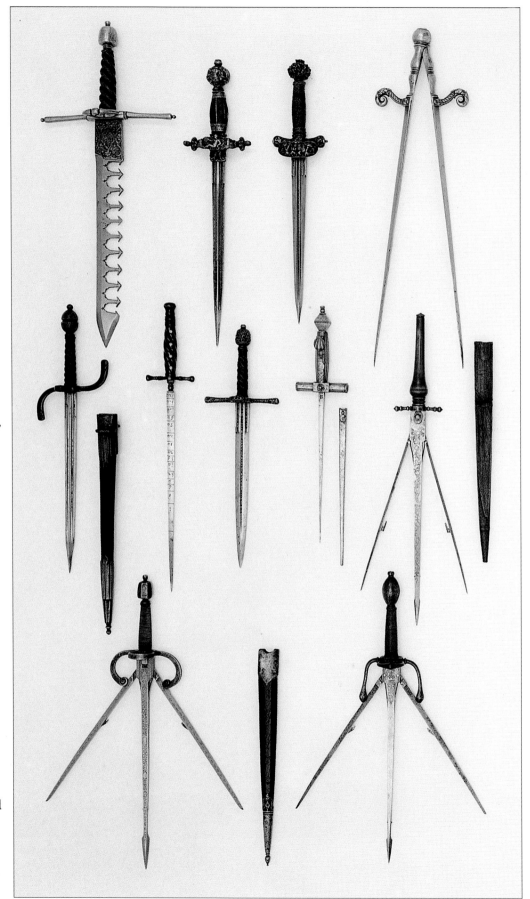

German boar spear of 1600 similar to those used in France. Large leaf-shaped blade has strong central rib and hexagonal socket wrought in one piece. Small metal cross-piece at socket prevents boar impaling itself too deeply on spear. Without this, the ferocious animal might slide up staff and cause injury to huntsman. Blade and socket length: 13.75 inches. THE WALLACE COLLECTION.

Knife/Dagger Type Bayonets

Later documentary and anecdotal evidence indicates that bayonets in more recognisable style possibly originated in France. This was in the vicinity of the town of Bayonne situated in the southwest of the country not far from the Spanish border. Bayonne had evidently been a thriving hub of cutlery and weapon manufacturing for many centuries. French crossbow-men called *baionners* apparently used to carry short swords. Cotgrave's *Dictionary* of 1611 refers to a 'bayonette' as a small flat pocket dagger furnished with knives, or a great knife to hang at the girdle, like a dagger.[2]

It also seems that the introduction of the bayonet may initially have related to boar hunting in the region, making it nec-

essary to examine briefly this hazardous activity. In the 17th century the hunting of this brave and ferocious animal was a popular Continental sport because of the excitement of the chase, and as a means of obtaining fresh and delicious meat. Huntsmen were equipped with hunting swords, daggers, boar spears, boar swords (see page 65), and early matchlock firearms. Spears comprised a very robust staff with strong, wide, leaf-shaped head incorporating a metal cross-piece (see picture). The purpose of the cross-piece was to allow rapid weapon withdrawal and prevent a wounded animal from climbing up the shaft and injuring the huntsman. A similar cross-piece was also mounted on boar sword blades. One legend states that a boar hunter who had only wounded a boar with his firearm was then confronted by the charging animal. Being defenceless, because his spear was out of reach, and lacking the time to reload, he thrust a dagger into the firearm muzzle in order to defend himself.

A second legend on the origin of the bayonet relates that some Basque countrymen were once pursuing brigands who had attacked their homes. When gunpowder and ammunition were exhausted, they thrust their sword hilts into the muskets, then charged and defeated the brigands. Further written theories are provided by Menage's *Dictionary* of 1694, and Voltaire's *Henriade*, written a hundred years later. Both suggest that the first bayonet was adapted from a crossbow-man's knife made in Bayonne.

Whatever the true cause, or reason, for the invention of the bayonet, we can probably accept the theory that it originated in, or near Bayonne, in about 1640.

The Plug Bayonet 1650-1690

The first bayonet was called a 'plug' because it was pushed into the muzzle of the firearm and retained in this manner thereafter, until removed to reload the matchlock musket. It seems the French, who were then the leading Continental military nation, were the first to adopt, and then adapt, the weapon for military purposes. The French historian, Maréchal de Puysegur, when describing his military experiences of 1647, stated that his soldiers carried bayonets with handles and blades each of a foot long. His classification description of the arm was as follows:

'a straight two-sided blade about a foot long, with tapered wooden hilt that could be inserted into a musket muzzle'. In the early 1660s it was used in the Low Countries by the British and other armies.'[3] The British army possessed some bayonets (which they received from the French) in 1662, and used them in Tangiers in 1663. Due to a lack of government money, and a conservative attitude towards untried new arms, it was probably not until about 1681 that the British army was issued with plug bayonets as a general issue.

Specifications

The plug bayonet was made in several forms for different purposes. Some were produced for sporting tasks and these can regularly be seen in contemporary pictures. Frequently they were of extremely high quality (see picture). Others were provided for members of the private guards of important personages. Finally, they were made in greater numbers for armies. The quality of these, although rightly of robust form, was actually surprisingly high, unlike the utilitarian military weapon horrors fashioned at the time. Most, including military patterns, had straight blades, whilst others, presumably hunting patterns, had curved ones. Apart from the blades, the design of all types was basically similar. The hilt of wood, ivory or horn/bone was circular and rather sharply tapered towards the pommel, enabling them to be inserted easily into the barrel muzzle. The sharp taper was particularly necessary because many contemporary muskets had bores of widely differing sizes. Therefore, the hilt design guaranteed that a bayonet would fit most available

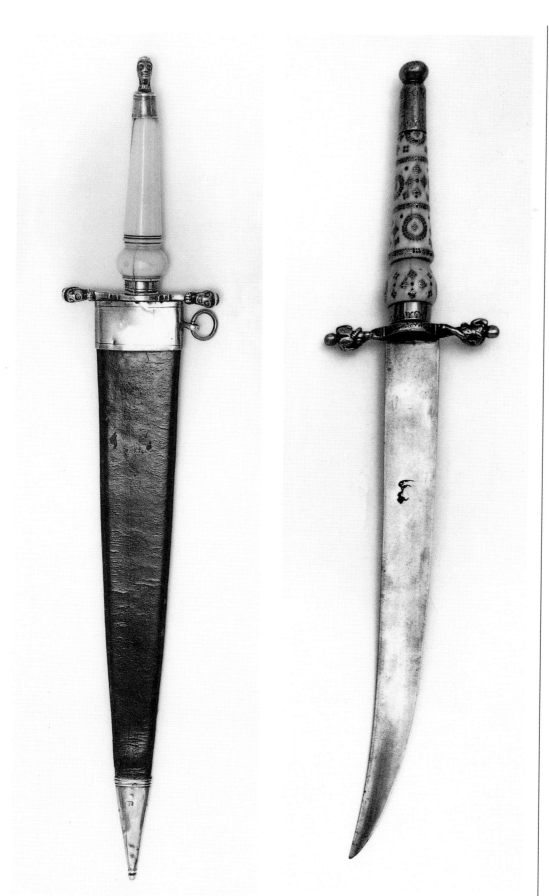

Left:
English plug bayonet of late 17th C. Plain, tapering, double-edged blade. Turned ivory grip with silver mounts and quillons with warriors' head terminals. Complete with silver mounted scabbard. Overall length: 17.5 inches.
COURTESY OF CHRISTIE, MANSON & WOOD.

Right:
High quality English plug bayonet, late 17th C, with overall length of 16 inches. Curved single-edged blade is stamped with maker's mark. Brass-mounted hilt decorated with punched dots and foliage with quillons formed as standing cherubs. Turned ivory grip inlaid with patterns of circles enriched with green dots.
COURTESY OF CHRISTIE, MANSON & WOOD.

firearms. The weapon had a neat, short cross-guard (like that of a Quillon dagger) with enlarged, frequently decorated, tips (see picture captions for detailed descriptions). Military models most often had straight, triangular, double-edged blades. Overall bayonet lengths varied from about 14 to 17 inches. The metal pommels were small and aligned with the tapering hilts. They were capped with a small, plain, spherical disk, or fashioned head. Bayonets were issued in a leather scabbard, which soldiers usually carried suspended from the waist belt.

Advantages and Disadvantages

In Chapter IV we shall examine the very signficant ways in which the introduction of the bayonet led to so many important military developments. At this point, it is sufficient to say that it enabled an infantryman to protect himself, to some degree at least, after he had discharged his musket and before the long, rather complicated reloading drill had been performed. Contemporarily, as we have noted, he depended upon pikemen to provide this during the vulnerable stage. However, the new weapon had several limitations. These were: once the bayonet was fitted to the matchlock the firearm could not be discharged; when the firearm was loaded the bayonet could not be fixed; if it was pushed too tightly into the muzzle it was difficult, or immediately impossible, to unfix; and if not pushed in firmly enough it might fall off the firearm, or remain in an opponent's body after a successful thrust. The problem of an insecure fix was, actually, one which bedevilled the bayonet throughout much of its history. There was also a tactical disadvantage for troops advancing with bayonets fixed because it indicated to the enemy either that their muskets were unloaded or, if loaded, they could not be fired without first unfixing the weapon.

Collectors should appreciate the rarity and significance of plug bayonets and make their inclusion in a collection a major ambition. Unfortunately, because of their scarcity, they are naturally expensive in relation to other bayonet patterns. They are also difficult to find. Nonetheless, examples do appear periodically in auction houses and less frequently at arms fairs. Collectors very keen to purchase might consider the rather drastic option of selling a good, but less rare, collection item partly to offset the higher price of a plug bayonet. After all, plug bayonets rarely come on the market and such opportunities should not be missed. They also provide a good long-term investment.

English military Plug bayonet of late 17th C. Straight, triangular double-edged blade with oblong ricasso. Straight brass quillons capped with helmeted heads and matching pommel. Tapering circular grip with brass ferrules. Overall length: 15 inches.
COURTESY OF CHRISTIE, MANSON & WOOD.

The Battle of Killiecrankie, 1689

This battle, fought between government troops and Jacobite supporters of the deposed King James II, occurred in Scotland. It was one of the first at which British troops were able properly to test plug bayonets under active service conditions. The Jacobites were generally armed with double-edged, basket hilted broadswords, the dirk, which we studied in Part I, and old-fashioned two-handed broadswords. The government commander was General Mackay, whose infantry troops were equipped with muskets and plug bayonets. The Jacobite commander was Viscount Claverhouse, referred to as 'Bonnie Dundee', on account of his long, black, curling locks. He was an excellent field commander, who delayed starting the battle until the strong evening sun had set and was no longer shining into the eyes of his men. He then ordered a downhill frontal charge towards the government army. As usual, this set off at a great pace with the momentum increased by the packed ranks. Despite significant casualties, caused by controlled volley fire, the clansmen reached the static regiments before the soldiers had time to fix their plug bayonets. The Highlanders cut, slashed and hacked their way through the ranks with clansmen sometimes killing, with dirk and broadsword, two soldiers simultaneously. Mackay's army, including the cavalry, disintegrated and dissolved in flight. This catastrophe, caused by the delay in fixing bayonets, subsequently prompted the British government to adopt a different bayonet pattern, called the ring bayonet, which had been invented by the French.

Notes

1 Montgomery of Alamein, *A History of Warfare*, Collins, London
2, 3 Howard L Blackmore, *Hunting Weapons*, Barrie & Jenkins

A rare German Boar-sword (Schwein-Degen), early 16th C. Straight, slender blade of 40 inches with later sprung cross-bar sited just above swelling tip of flattened diamond section.

REPRODUCED BY COURTESY OF CHRISTIE, MANSON & WOODS.

Chapter II

THE EVOLUTION OF LATER BAYONETS

British soldier at Namur in 1695 *from an original painting by B. Fosten. Note his equipment: flintlock musket, plug bayonet and sword. The bayonet in leather scabbard is attached to the waist belt.*
REPRODUCED BY COURTESY OF THE EDITOR OF THE QUEEN'S ROYAL SURREY REGIMENT ASSOCIATION NEWSLETTER.

Ring Bayonets

The ring bayonet was invented to incorporate two, new, excellent ideas. The first was to achieve a firmer, more reliable attachment to the musket; the second, to allow the firearm to be loaded and discharged when the bayonet was fixed. Successful achievement of this naturally saved the considerable time which had previously been devoted to bayonet fixing and unfixing. In this pattern, the bayonet was attached to the musket barrel with two circular, loose, metal rings which slipped over both the bayonet hilt and the firearm muzzle. This, in theory at least, afforded the advantages of being able both to load and fire, with the bayonet fixed, with the result that soldiers were immediately ready to defend themselves after firing. However, despite the evolutionary importance of the new bayonet principles, the attachment system was unsuccessful in practice because bayonets still frequently fell off the barrels.

Ring bayonets had been used by the

French, on a trial basis, for some eleven years. Maréchal de Puysegur mentioned that at least one French regiment was furnished with a comparable pattern in 1678. When the French decided the ring bayonet was unsuitable, they researched and introduced another weapon form. It is of interest that the French, whose army was then the best on the Continent, seemed to undertake most of the early bayonet development research.

Split-Socket Bayonets

The French army were issued with the new bayonet during 1703-4. It incorporated a round hilt, in socket form, into the side of which was a right-angled slot extending to the open end of the socket tube. The bayonet was passed over the musket sight (very rudimentary at this time) and locked with a half turn.[1] This pattern was devised by Lt Colonel J Martinet who was inspector of infantry in the army of Louis XIV. The open-ended socket allowed the bayonet to be squeezed onto large bore barrels as well as fitting smaller bore barrels. At last, the French succeeded in producing an effective bayonet which enabled them to advance infantry formations with fixed bayonets, then, when appropriate, to halt, fire a volley, and at once attack with the bayonet alone. 'However, it was not until the French army had gained victories with this new form of weapon that it was adopted by other armies, including the British.'[2]

The split-socket bayonet, in a variety of forms, continued in use until the early 18th century.

It is worth mentioning an extremely unusual bayonet which resulted from French technical weapon development. This was a very high quality, triple-bladed plug bayonet (see picture page 68) of about 1660. The design must have been influenced by the principles incorporated in left-hand triple-bladed daggers, used with the rapier, to catch and perhaps break an opponent's blade. When the stud on the ricasso (sited just below the cross guard) was pulled back, it released two additional blades which automatically sprang out. This exceptionally well-fashioned and decorated weapon can be seen in The Wallace Collection (acc No: A 866). Collectors are recommended to see this arm after they have studied the magnificent dagger collection in an adjacent gallery.

Drawing of a ring bayonet of about 1689. From engraving in Grose's Military Antiquities.

The Common Fixed Socket Bayonet

This plain, strong, and simple pattern was introduced about 1730. Unlike the earlier socket bayonet, introduced by the French, which had an open-ended socket, this had a closed socket end in the form of a raised, round, circular collar. In form, it consisted of a triangular shaped blade with two deeply fullered side sections and flat top joined by a curved shoulder to a closed socket. This comprised a short, round tube with its raised collar at the end. A zig-zag slot was cut into the tube side. To fix the bayonet, the tube was slipped over the muzzle and the zig-zag slot fitted and locked onto a stud on the barrel. Again, these bayonets did sometimes fall off, but the problem occurred less often than with the ring bayonet. Subsequent British patterns had a slightly curved blade top (see picture). Even these had a propensity periodically to fall off the barrel. This bayonet, in numerous forms, was adopted by Continental nations. It should be appreciated that the pattern could only be used in

Extremely rare high quality triple-bladed plug bayonet on display at The Wallace Collection (acc No: 866). An ingenious weapon, probably French, of about 1660. Note tapering horn grip swelling towards quillons topped with small brass caps. Stud on ricasso which, when pulled back, releases two additional side blades which automatically spring out. This device was influenced by similar ones in some left-hand daggers, used with a rapier about 1590 to 1630. Overall length: 19 inches, blade length: 13.2 inches.

THE WALLACE COLLECTION.

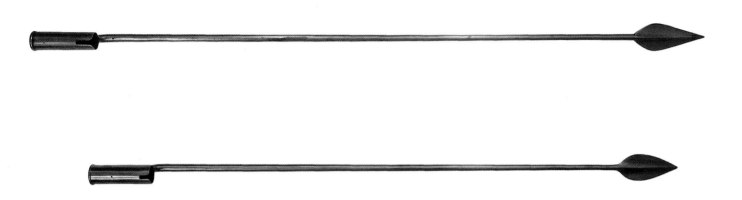

combat to produce straight thrusting and stabbing strokes. (See picture page 74)

To avoid classification confusion among collectors, it is worth mentioning that the British Brown Bess bayonet was issued in several shorter forms. Sergeants were issued with a 13-inch bladed model; cadets an 8-inch one, and a 15-inch pattern was used on the carbine musket. Examples of these appear at arms fairs and should be snapped up once they have been convincingly identified.

Socket bayonets were subsequently produced by many nations in a rather confusing profusion. These continued in service until the late 19th century. For example, a long pattern for the Martini-Enfield rifle (1833), and a short socket one for the Martini-Henry rifle (1871). Many incorporated additional locking rings and spring attachment fasteners to achieve an ever more secure attachment to a firearm. The author has often found it difficult to identify some of these immediately. He can recommend the excellent *British Military Bayonets* by R J Wilkinson Latham, which provides great assistance with British patterns.

Our next chapter is devoted to the evolution of early hand-held weapons from the late 15th century to 1700. This is necessary because the bayonet eventually became an integral and mandatory partner of the long firearm making it relevant for us to study the development of the matchlock, flintlock, and percussion operated firearms. It was the partnership of an improved new firearm, plus an efficient bayonet, which eventually made possible such important military changes. Readers with detailed knowledge of firearms may prefer to go directly to Chapter IV which explains the effects of the bayonet upon military history.

Two British bayonets of 18th C.

Top: For cavalry carbine, with small leaf shaped blade with long steel shank connected to simple tubular socket with L-shaped slot to take foresight block. When not in use the bayonet can be reversed on carbine, the point engaging in a slot in front of the trigger guard. Overall length: 29 inches, blade length: 26 inches.

Bottom: The example is a similar socket bayonet of 1736-6.

(NEG NO: A4/191)
THE BOARD OF TRUSTEES OF THE ROYAL ARMOURIES.

Notes

1, 2 R J Wilkinson Latham, *British Military Bayonets*, Hutchinson, London.

Chapter III

EARLY FIREARMS

Hand Gunner of 1470
PICTURE BY D W WORTHY ESQ.

It is of interest now briefly to examine infantry firearms from the 15th to the late 17th century. This is because some understanding of them, and their effectiveness and limitations, makes it easier to appreciate bayonet importance.

The Hand-Culverin: Late 15th Century

This firearm succeeded the unpredictable Hand Gun, or Hand Gonne, in about 1470. The term is used to classify numerous firearms of similar type, but of differing sizes, patterns, and names. They all weighed between 12 and 20 pounds, with barrel lengths up to about 3.5 feet. The new weapons were operated by two men. The senior carried the culverin and was responsible for its combat loading and aiming. The second helped with transporting the piece and carrying bullets and powder. After a hand-culverin was loaded, the following firing procedure took place: the senior man used both hands to hold the weapon whilst aiming it at a suitable target; once he wished to fire, he told the second man, who then ignited the charge at the barrel touch hole with a lighted brand. Despite its clumsy appearance, slow rate of fire and awkward firing procedures, this weapon, like the previous hand-gun, possessed two extremely important attributes – the ability to penetrate plate armour at ranges of between 50 and 100 yards, thus directly contributing to the final stage of armoured cavalry obsolescence, and, more important, the realisation that firearms made all men equal in war and transformed the effectiveness of foot soldiers.

The Matchlock Arquebus: Early 16th Century

The next firearm was the much more effective arquebus developed in about 1500. This was the first firearm remotely to resemble rifles of the 19th century. It was far superior to previous arms such as the hand-gun, and the clumsy two-man culverin, being lighter, with shorter butt, longer barrel and smaller bore. The much improved new piece could, therefore, be more easily held by a soldier against his shoulder and so was more accurate. A second soldier was not needed to assist in the firing process. But the success of the arquebus was mainly due to the adoption of a technologically advanced new ignition system, the operation of which only required the use of one finger to activate it. This enabled the weapon to be held and steadied with both hands. The ignition system incorporated a long, smouldering match which was retained by a cock on a swivelling serpentine. 'The match was a loosely twisted rope of hemp that had been dipped in saltpetre and spirits of wine, so that it would burn slowly.'[1] The serpentine was: 'a device for attaching the match to the gun. A clamp was fashioned in one end of a strip of metal bent in the form of the letter S'[2]. This was connected to a trigger sited underneath the arm near the stock. To fire, the soldier aimed at the target then, when ready, pulled the trigger which moved the serpentine, and also the cock and burning match, onto the priming pan. The priming charge was thus ignited. This, in turn, caused the explosion of the main charge which fired the weapon. The only problem with this procedure was the pause between squeezing the trigger and the actual detonation of the main charge. Doubtless this was disconcerting to the intended target! The most important advantage of the arquebus was that it enabled the soldier to concentrate fully upon aiming because the ignition was now performed automatically. This naturally resulted in much improved accuracy. Eventually the efficiency of the arquebus caused its adoption by most European nations. The first general to appreciate the inherent possibilities of the arquebus was Gonzalo de Cordoba in about 1496. He consequently greatly increased the number of arquebusiers in his army.

German matchlock musket c1560, of 0.8 inch calibre, barrel length 42.5 inches and weight 13lbs 8ozs.
(NEG NO: A4/190)
THE BOARD OF TRUSTEES OF THE ROYAL ARMOURIES.

German matchlock arquebus c1600 of 1 inch calibre with a barrel length of 69.25 inches and weighing 44lbs 10ozs. Note upright aperture of back sight and recoil block below barrel. Pan cover and flash guard missing.
(NEG NO: A6/747)
THE BOARD OF TRUSTEES OF THE ROYAL ARMOURIES.

The Musket

This arm was introduced after the arquebus. It incorporated the match ignition system and could fire greater distances with more precision. But, it was considerably heavier than the arquebus and so was provided with a forked rest. Also, it had the further disadvantage 'of having a firing rate appreciably slower than the forty rounds an hour of the arquebus'[3]. In about 1580, 'the Spaniards had only 15 musketeers to a hundred arquebusiers, but by 1600 the proportions in most armies were about level'.[4]

General Firearm Improvements

Improvements were made slowly but regularly. On some patterns the trigger was replaced by a button which, when squeezed, released a catch causing the serpentine to fall forward and down onto the pan, instantly igniting the priming charge. This meant that the gun could be fired with a light pressure enabling the majority of the right hand to be used to hold and support the firearm. The position of the serpentine was then reversed so that it fell forwards towards the soldier rather than away from him. This enabled the firer automatically to check that the match was burning properly and in the correct position. Triggers were then reintroduced that were smaller than hitherto and protected by a guard. The early form of stocks were straight. These were rested on the shoulder, compelling the soldier to control the firing recoil with his arms and hands unless the arm was fitted with a recoil block sited beneath the barrel. New stocks had sharply curved butts held against the chest enabling better firearm control. This change caused more of the recoil force to be directed upwards making possible a gun in lighter form. The butts of Spanish guns were eventually broadened which allowed them to be held against the shoulder as they are today.

Three Italian matchlock muskets c1540.
(NEG NO: A13/330)
THE BOARD OF TRUSTEES
OF THE ROYAL ARMOURIES.

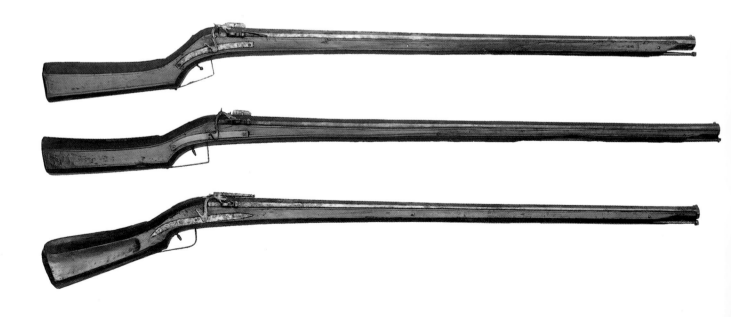

Caliver man from Jacob de Gheyn's Maniement d'Armes, *1608 which set down the methods of loading, priming and firing early matchlocks using step-by-step illustrations. This is only one illustration from a complete sequence.*

The Flint-lock Musket

About the middle of the 17th century, a most significant firearm improvement was introduced. This was a novel ignition system called the flint-lock. It comprised a steel striking plate, which also acted as a pan cover (to keep the priming charge dry), and a spring actuated cock which held in a piece of buff leather a neatly fashioned fragment of flint. The loading system of the flint-lock was thus easier and quicker than hitherto. A soldier was issued with about forty to sixty cartridges carried in leather pouches. Cartridges contained gunpowder and a round lead ball (bullet). To load, the soldier bit the end off the cartridge and poured a little powder into the priming pan which was then closed with the striking plate. The rest of the powder was poured down the barrel. The bullet and cartridge paper was then pushed gently down the barrel with a ramrod. Cartridge paper acted as wadding and thus slightly increased compression. To fire, the cock was pulled back and retained in the ready (cocked) position. When the trigger was squeezed it caused the hammer to fall forward and the flint to strike the bottom of the pan cover (striking plate). Reaction of flint on steel created a spark which ignited the priming powder in the flash

Brown Bess musket issued to 'The Warrington Blue Backs'. Note excellent design of beautifully crafted stock with its neat grip and crown cypher.

pan. A flame passed down the touch hole and ignited the main powder charge within the bore. The resulting explosion forced the bullet (ball) up and out of the barrel.

This clever and efficient invention revolutionised hand-held firearms. Flint-lock firearms made the matchlock obsolete. The system was soon adopted by all European nations in their standard issue firearms. 'Having a more reliable detonating device, it functioned better in wet weather and gave a higher rate of fire.'[5]. It was to these flint-lock operated firearms that the bayonet was then attached. From about 1700 infantry were equipped with the flint-lock musket, bayonet and short sword or hanger. The continued retention of the latter is rather surprising but was, perhaps, regarded as a safety precaution in case further bayonet fixing problems continued to be encountered.

The Brown Bess Musket

It may be of interest to readers, particularly British ones, briefly to examine a famous flint-lock musket which was employed by the British army for some 150 years. Very similar patterns of this firearm were contemporarily in service with many other nations.

The Brown Bess was a smooth bore, flint-lock operated military musket made general issue to the British army in 1730. It was notable for its graceful lines, functional brass fittings, and good balance. The name originates from either the browning process, which protected the barrel, or the word 'Bess' stemming from the German word '*büchse*' for tube, or gun. It had a bore of about .75 of an inch. This was larger than the bullet size which was either .70 or .72 of an inch. During its service it was made in eight slightly differing patterns. Initially, the barrel length was 46 inches; by the mid-18th century this was reduced to 42 inches. The musket was fitted with a wooden, brass-tipped ramrod later replaced by a more efficient one of steel. To the musket was fitted the triangular, fixed socket bayonet. This was retained when not in use in a triangular, leather-

Brown Bess musket fixed socket bayonet made by Dawes of Birmingham c1750. Note pronounced zig-zag slot.
AUTHOR'S COLLECTION.

Brown Bess muskets
From left to right:

Short land musket

Light infantry musket with 39 inch barrel.

Sergeant's carbine
New land pattern (1802) with actual issue date of 1832. These were produced by converting Light Infantry muskets.

Junior cadet carbine
issued to gentlemen cadets of the junior department of the Royal Military College. Only twenty were made.

(NEG NO: A5778/41)
THE BOARD OF TRUSTEES
OF THE ROYAL ARMOURIES.

covered scabbard tipped with brass chape and locket. Some patterns were adapted to fire grenades; these were used by grenadiers.

Combat discharge rate was about two rounds per minute. This was slow because all soldiers fired together to achieve a concerted volley which naturally involved waiting for the slowest loading soldier. Firing rate was about four rounds per minute if soldiers omitted priming the pan. Instead, the full contents of the cartridge powder charge was poured down the barrel, and the butt banged on the ground, which hopefully primed the pan in the reverse manner. So, although a faster loading method, it did cause more misfires. The weapon was accurate up to sixty yards and moderately so up to 100 yards. Above this it was very inaccurate.

Because the performance of all European firearms was fairly similar (except rifles), contemporary tactics were realistically developed which did not demand a high accuracy rate. Consequently, it mattered little if a soldier hit the target at which he aimed or another ten yards away. British infantry tactics were often based on linear formations (thin red lines) which allowed more soldiers to fire simultaneously. These made possible a larger number of bullets being volley fired at once whilst presenting a smaller mass target to the enemy. During the Seven Years War (1756-63), Frederick the Great devised a rather risky but most effective new formation. 'To gain maximum fire-power he deployed his army in the thinnest lines any general had yet dared to use.'[6] Good fire discipline (means of firmly controlling soldiers' fire) was achieved by constant arms and foot drill with the purpose of achieving fast, concerted volleys at close range. These, if successful, compensated for inferior weaponry. All battlefield movement, and particularly musketry loading and firing, were very closely supervised to ensure rapid and cohesive battlefield action.

The great victories of the Duke of Marlborough at Blenheim (1704), Ramillies (1706), and Malplaquet (1709) were to a large degree achieved by the skill with which British soldiers handled their muskets and bayonets.

Notes

1, 2 Harold L Peterson, *The Book of the Gun*, Paul Hamlyn, London.
3, 4, 5 Montgomery of Alamein, *A History of Warfare*, Collins.
6 Paul Kendal, *The Story of Land Warfare*, Hamish Hamilton.

Chapter IV

HOW BAYONETS INFLUENCED WARFARE

The grand old Duke of York, he had 10,000 men, he marched them
up to the top of the hill and he marched them down again!

Introduction

In about 1600, armies comprised large units of pikemen, detachments of arquebusiers and musketeers, cavalry and muzzle loading artillery. Cavalry were attempting to regain some status after the obsolescence of the heavily armoured knight. To achieve this they generally chose firearms, and many were armed with the wheel-lock pistol, invented in Austria about 1545. These were activated by a sophisticated device which operated rather like a clockwork cigarette lighter. A powerful main spring was unwound causing a steel wheel to revolve against a piece of iron pyrites (later flint). This created sparks which ignited the powder charge. Wheel-locks were frequently of very high quality and often elaborately decorated. Many had rifled barrels making them accurate up to about fifty paces. Horsemen used them in caracole tactics. This involved squadrons advancing upon the enemy and firing their pistols by rank, at close range, then wheeling away to the rear to reload. All six squadron ranks would repeat this process in turn. German Reiters were the most famous cavalry to employ these tactics.

Pikemen

Units of pikemen served in all 17th century armies. They were often very large, containing over 4,000 men each, and resembling huge hedgehogs. They were rather unwieldy and somewhat difficult to control, particularly when a change of direction was dictated on the march. However, once advancing into the attack, or when holding a static defensive position, they could often defeat cavalry, and sometimes opposing pikemen units, due to their formation stolidity and the length and density of the pikes. They usually, but not always, kept horsemen at a distance. Each rank held their pikes at a different level which presented an intimidating display of glittering blades. They also provided a useful counter-attack force. Improved firearms resulted in the creation of small units of semi-independent infantry. Pikemen formations were given extra responsibility for providing them with protection. This was particularly so during the long and vulnerable reloading process. This custom continued for a long time until the eventual appearance of better firearms, fitted with bayonets which did not fall off the barrels so often.

***Two open, split-socket bayonets**, both probably British, early 18th C.*

Top: overall length: 15.5 inches, blade: 11.4 inches, weight 12ozs.

Bottom: overall length: 18.5 inches, blade: 13.5 inches, weight 14ozs.

(NEG NO: A6/998)
THE BOARD OF TRUSTEES OF
THE ROYAL ARMOURIES.

The Bayonet

In Chapter III we saw how the infantry adoption of the much more dependable flint-lock musket greatly improved firing speed. Firearms-bearing foot soldiers became more effective and efficient, which increased their usefulness and status. Their military establishments were increased in consequence.

The introduction of the bayonet, although initially accidental, did present army commanders with the chance to develop further the improved efficiency and independence of their infantry arm. However, as we appreciate, the problems caused by faulty attachment mechanisms on the plug and ring patterns postponed the achievement of their objectives. But, once the more reliable common fixed socket bayonet was developed and fitted to the technologically advanced flint-lock musket, the prerequisites for major military changes were in place. These changes were: the transformation of the types of units within an army; greater unit mobility, and the opportunity for commanders to deploy and manoeuvre their forces much more quickly and easily than previously.

Changes in Army Units

Flint-lock muskets and common socket bayonets provided the means whereby infantrymen could now perform two essential tasks on their own. These were: to deliver effectively controlled volley fire which could defeat cavalry, other firearm equipped infantry and pikemen; and provide their own defence after muskets had been fired. The bayonet was essential for the accomplishment of both of these. Success in all the tasks depended upon well disciplined soldiers. This naturally resulted in pikemen being obsolete. Gradually, therefore, fewer pikemen units were employed in armies until, by about 1700, they had disappeared from the battlefield. This major change was compensated for by the recruitment of far more infantry units called regiments, or battalions. These were very much smaller than the pikemen units, comprising only between 600 and 700 men each. From about 1700, infantry equipped with flintlock musket and bayonet created more mobile, flexible and semi-independent units. The bayonet was one of the essential equipment items which made these radical changes possible.

Greater Unit Mobility

Because infantrymen no longer carried the burning match to detonate their firearms, or shouldered a musket rest to support the early musket, they were far less encumbered than hitherto. The possession of the bayonet also enabled the sword or hanger to be discarded. Soldiers in the new regiments were now regularly drilled to ensure immediate and cohesive unit movement. Consequently, both they, and the units in which they served, could be rapidly and simply moved around the battlefield to be deployed in more tactically advantageous positions. Foot soldiers could now strike rapid and effective blows in the attack as well as from a defensive position. This was a radical military change; 'mobility, and the reliance on firepower rather than shock, increased the possibility of good troops winning against numerical odds'[1]. Warfare had become much more regimented, mobile and flexible.

Commanders' Control of their Armies

Cavalry tactics also changed. The slow and potentially hazardous caracole tactics, relying upon the wheel-lock pistol, were replaced by new ones introduced by Gustavus Adolphus of Sweden. The sword became the principal weapon, with pistols retained for use in the close-quarter melee. The final stage of a cavalry charge was performed at the gallop. Consequently, the speed and weight of cavalry was once again utilised to achieve shock power. By reverting to the use of such tactics cavalry once again became formidable.

As both cavalry and infantry now had the ability and proven procedures to move rapidly either into the attack or to deploy to favourable defensive locations, a commander's options were far greater. Therefore, generals were able quickly to implement much more ambitious tactical manoeuvres and consequently achieved decisive battle results more frequently.

Army Training

During the Middle Ages, the training of the 'regular' troops such as the armoured knight, crossbowman and longbowman was a very lengthy process. The knight had to be brave, physically tough, an excellent rider, and accustomed to wearing uncomfortable protective accoutrements. Eventually, he became skilled at executing his primary role of handling his warhorse and weapons to achieve the maximum shock power in the charge, This was an extremely difficult skill and took several years to perfect, involving endless practice in the tilt yard. He also had to master the correct handling of weapons, in particular the sword. The English longbowman started his training and the development of his physique at the age of eight. By seventeen he was adequately competent. Crossbowmen also took several years to acquire satisfactory marksmanship skills. By the end of the 17th century, science had made things much easier for the soldier through the development of efficient firearms. It no longer required years of arduous training to become a competent foot soldier because they only had to master the techniques of handling a fairly simple and efficient firearm, and learning foot drill. Both these responsibilities could be adequately mastered in about twelve weeks. Therefore whole armies of fairly capable troops could be mustered very quickly. Consequently, commanders tended to lead much bigger armies than hitherto and could be reinforced with fresh troops fairly rapidly. As Napoleon later stated: 'God is on the side of the bigger battalions.'

Notes

1 Montgomery of Alamein, *A History of Warfare*, Collins.

Chapter V

MUSKET, BAYONET, FIFE AND DRUM

1730-1830

'You may do anything with Bayonets except sit on them': Napoleon

Contemporary Warfare

Throughout this period, warfare was dominated by the musket and the bayonet. Well drilled infantry advanced in line or column, defended in company formations, or formed hollow squares when attacked by cavalry. The predominant theory of infantry formations was that thinner and longer ranks enabled more soldiers to fire simultaneously at the enemy whilst providing less tempting targets. The risk of such an arrangement was that a weakly held line might not prevent penetration by enemy cavalry or footmen. The bayonet was used to repel assaults by opposing horsemen and foot soldiers by presenting an intimidating array of gleaming blades and volley fire. In the attack it was employed to finish off an enemy after their ranks had already been thinned by devastating concerted musket fire. It may be asked why, with muskets providing such slow and inaccurate fire, regiments did not immediately attack with the bayonet. The reason was the effect of volley fire at very close range which, when well controlled, delivered fire by one rank at a time. This often caused extremely high casualties.

The prerequisite of successful volley fire was to delay opening fire upon an advancing enemy until the last possible moment. This ensured that the maximum number of bullets struck a target. It required commanding officers to have strong nerves and the soldiers great courage. Hence the famous order: 'don't fire until you see the whites of their eyes'.

In the 18th century regiments presented a magnificent spectacle in battle – clad in colourful uniforms, bearing highly polished muskets fitted with glittering bayonets, and with every movement controlled by precise and complicated drill. Soldiers' stature was frequently enhanced by tall and elaborate hats, and the wearing of packs above the shoulders. Music produced by brass bands was also important as it helped to maintain morale and increase advance momentum, whilst the repetitive sound had a slightly mesmeric effect which dulled fear. Drummer boys maintained this momentum at company level.

Flint-lock rifle. American. Pennsylvania, c1760. Prototype of the Kentucky rifle.
(ACC NO: XII, 1456)
THE BOARD OF TRUSTEES
OF THE ROYAL ARMOURIES.

The American War of Independence 1775-83

It is appropriate to examine battlefield events in this war because of the major difference between the small arms used by the protagonists. British infantry employed the Brown Bess musket and socket bayonet, whilst their adversaries often carried rifles. The influence of the latter was to have some impact upon bayonet evolution.

Initially, American pioneers used robust, heavy sporting rifles, such as the Jaeger, which they had brought with them from Germany. It will be appreciated that in the interior a good rifle, and the ability to handle it efficiently, were vital to survival. Designed to hunt deer, wild boar and chamois, it was also no doubt used to kill large, local animals such as bears. These heavy muzzle-loading weapons used bullets of 16-20 in the pound. In the Eastern states of the new country, however, there were far less large, dangerous game. Therefore, rifles were slowly adapted to conform to local conditions where hunting mostly involved the shooting of game birds and deer. These arms, many of which were made in Pennsylvania, were usually fixed-sight rifles with longer barrels and smaller bores firing lighter, patched bullets of 40 in the pound. The patch of greased doe skin or rag, in which the bullet was wrapped, ensured a greater spin of the bullet, whilst increasing gun compression. The barrels gradually became longer, extending to 38 or 40 inches. With these arms the Americans were able to hit targets, including moving animals, at up to 300 yards. Such game shooting provided excellent training for the subsequent war against the British redcoats. 'They could fire with faultless precision from any stance but preferred the prone position.'[1] Combined with their excellent field craft skills, and dull coloured clothing which afforded good camouflage, it is not surprising that the backwoodsmen regularly discomfited British troops. Armed with their very high quality rifles, the Americans were superb infantrymen.

Detail of Flint-lock rifle, American, Pennsylvania, c1760. The prototype of the Kentucky rifle.
Calibre: 45ins
Barrel length: 45ins
Weight: 8lbs, 5oz

(ACC NO: XII. 1456)
THE BOARD OF TRUSTEES
OF THE ROYAL ARMOURIES.

During the war combat success depended upon ground scenarios. On open battlefields the British generally defeated the colonist militiamen by their use of parade ground drilled movement and well controlled rapid firing rolling volleys. In close, broken country where fighting was most likely to involve conflict, 'between man and man, and on the shoot-when-you-meet principle, the odds were as heavily in favour of the Americans, as being beyond comparison the better individual marksman'[2]. The lessons of the American rifles naturally created a lasting impression on the British. This led to a brave and resourceful officer, Captain P Ferguson, who was an expert shot, designing his own weapon based on the Chaumette breech loading rifle. This became known as the Ferguson rifle. The excellent arm could accurately fire six shots per minute at 200 yards which was much faster than the Brown Bess musket. The latter, plus experiences in the American war, led to the British production of the new Baker rifle in 1801.

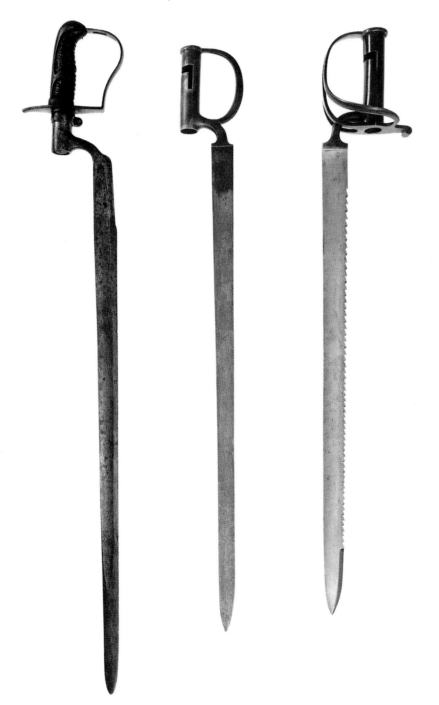

Three unusual bayonets.

Left: This bayonet has a detachable hilt. The sword socket pattern is associated with the Cambridge University volunteers. It has a Knock type locking ring similar to that found on the Duke of Richmond's pattern musket and Baker socket bayonet 1796. Example shown dated 1798.

Middle: Volunteer sword socket bayonet (pattern 1790) similar to the Sappers & Miners bayonet. The bayonet fits by means of a normal slot and bar to a volunteer pattern Baker rifle manufactured by Wallis of Birmingham, dated 1805.

Right: A first pattern Sappers & Miners bayonet for the Sappers' carbine. It is dated 1842 and is believed to be the only existing example as this pattern never went into production.

(NEG NO: A4/196)
THE BOARD OF TRUSTEES
OF THE ROYAL ARMOURIES.

The Baker Rifle

This was introduced for several reasons: the decision to recruit several riflemen units to serve in the Peninsular War and the continuation of the British army tradition of maintaining several rifle regiments providing at least some soldiers who could accurately fire at longer ranges than was possible with the musket. Previously, the army had recruited Continental rifle regiments, on a secondment basis, to fulfil this role. Finally, uncomfortable memories of the American War of Independence, in particular the splendid marksmanship of the backwoodsmen, and Captain Ferguson's rifle, also influenced the government ruling. The technical performance of this rifle may be of particular interest to wargamers who specialise in the Napoleonic War battles.

The French army also learned similar lessons from this war. Immediately after their revolution they set up units of rifle carrying sharpshooters. In the attack, these light infantrymen (*tirailleurs*) with accurate, long-range rifles, advanced forward of the main army acting as sharpshooters and skirmishers. They would move to a vantage point, out of range of hostile musket fire, and shoot an enemy officer, then move rapidly to the next point and repeat the process. They were very successful at causing disruption and uncertainty in opposing frontal formations. Doubtless, the success of these also prompted the creation of similar British troops who served in what became known as the Rifle Brigade.

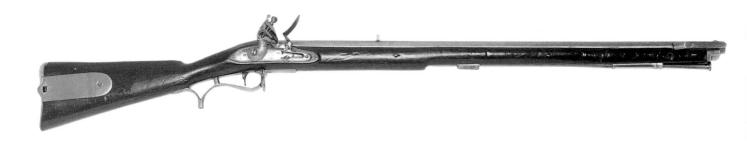

The flint-lock operated, muzzle-loading Baker rifle.
THE CURATOR, WEAPONS COLLECTION, HQ SMALL ARMS SCHOOL CORPS.

Specifications

This short flint-lock-operated, muzzle-loading rifle was designed by Ezekiel Baker of London and was retained in service for about thirty-seven years. It had a browned barrel 2 feet 6 inches long with bore of .615 of an inch. The rifle weighed 9.5 pounds and was sighted up to 100 yards with an additional leaf sight calibrated up to 200 yards. The leaf sight was subsequently discarded and replaced with a fixed sight set at 200 yards. To load, a correct powder charge, measured by a gadget on the powder horn, was poured down the barrel; a bullet wrapped in a piece of greased cloth was next pushed down the barrel with the ram rod. Patches were retained in a box on the stock. Bullets used were of 20 rounds in the pound. The rifleman carried a powder horn, bullets, pricker to clear the touch hole, and a small brush to clean the pan. Baker selected a cleverly thought-out type of rifling. It deliberately only had a small degree of twist designed to reduce friction between the bullet and the inside of the barrel, ensuring simpler loading because: 'the Baker ball was designed to drop down the bore of its own weight if loaded without the greased patch'[3]. The second considerable firing advantage was that the arm managed 'to secure a flat trajectory for the ball during the first two or three hundred yards of flight'[4].

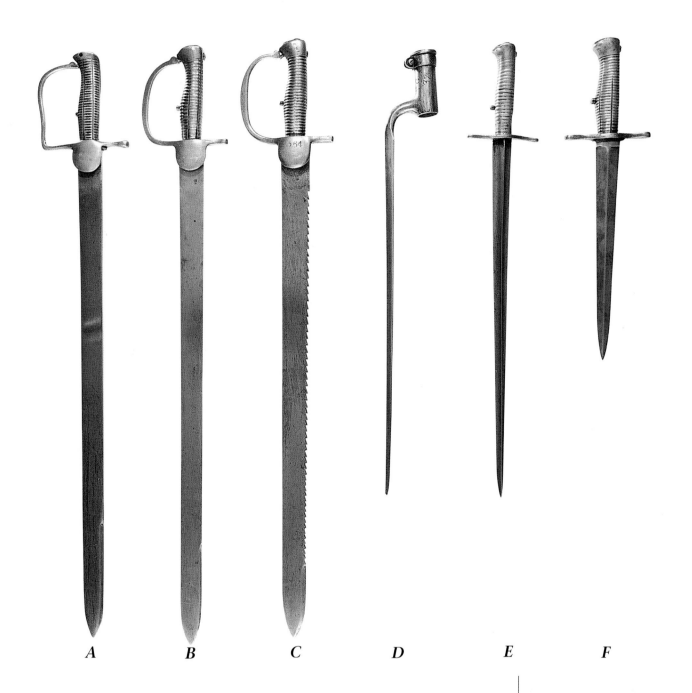

Baker Rifle Bayonets.
A. Sword bayonet, 1800,
first pattern.
B. Sword bayonet, 1801,
second pattern.
C. Experimental saw back
bayonet, 1801.
D. Socket bayonet, 1815.
E. Hand pattern, 1823.
F. Experimental Hand
pattern 'trench knife'.
(NEG NO. A5430/12)
THE BOARD OF TRUSTEES
OF THE ROYAL ARMOURIES.

Firing Rate and Range

This was about two rounds per minute when carefully loaded with the greased patch and correctly calibrated powder charge (that is, ensuring that the full amount of powder specified by the horn calibrator was actually poured into the barrel). If the patch was not used, the firing rate was naturally much higher. Such a course, although useful at close quarters, would have been rather self-defeating because the weapon purpose was to achieve very accurate fire out of range of the opposition. The rifle was extremely accurate at up to 200 yards, and was very accurate up to about 300 yards. Beyond this it might still hit a mass target such as a company. The bayonet used with this firearm, including the experimental patterns, are of the greatest significance and interest.

The Bayonets

The Baker rifle was produced in several models. It was unusual because it used five different bayonet types. These were: the first pattern sword bayonet (1800) with rectangular brass knuckle bow and 23-inch blade, the second pattern (1801) with rounded brass-knuckle bow and 23-inch blade, a socket bayonet (1815) with 17-inch blade, the first hand pattern bayonet (1823) with 17-inch blade, and the second hand pattern (1826) with 17-inch blade. The two hand pattern models could also be used as daggers. Two additional experimental models were: the second pattern sword bayonet with a saw back, and a short hand bayonet with a 10.5-inch blade which could also provide a most handy dagger or 'trench' knife. The Baker was one of the first rifles to be equipped with sword bayonets which was a notable development. This pattern we examine in detail in Chapter VI.

All the Baker bayonets are of exceptional interest and the short hand models are particularly rare. Collectors are strongly recommended to acquire examples of any type offered for sale.

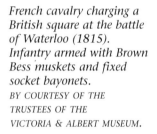

French cavalry charging a British square at the battle of Waterloo (1815). Infantry armed with Brown Bess muskets and fixed socket bayonets.
BY COURTESY OF THE TRUSTEES OF THE VICTORIA & ALBERT MUSEUM.

Notes

1, 2, 3, 4 J N George, *English Guns and Rifles*, Small-Arms Technical Publishing Company, Plantersville, South Carolina.

Chapter VI

THE SWORD BAYONET

We continue the bayonet story shortly after the battle of Waterloo (1815) where most soldiers upon the field were equipped with a musket and socket bayonet. The King's German Legion, however, used the Baker rifle and sword bayonet. This major battle was, perhaps, the high point in combat use of the flint-lock musket and socket bayonet, as improved technology was soon to create radical firearm changes. British infantry, which at the battle crisis was under extreme pressure from the excellent French artillery, was additionally subjected to repeated powerful cavalry attacks. Nonetheless, by forming defensive squares which presented a hedge of bayonets, they generally managed to withstand the horsemen in this vital battle; 'where French cavalry charged repeatedly at the wrong time, in the wrong manner, and on the wrong ground'[1].

The early 19th century was memorable for the upsurge of industrial technology, new scientific understanding, particularly of chemistry, and ingenious inventiveness. The trend generated significant firearm changes particularly relating to an advanced ignition method. This was the percussion cap which eventually resulted from the efforts of several clever inventors. It comprised a hollow metal cap containing a priming mixture. This was placed on a hollow nipple connected to the main charge within the barrel bore. The flint holding lock was replaced by a neat hammer one. On squeezing the trigger the hammer came forward and struck the cap, the explosion of which ignited the main charge and fired the weapon. This system was much more reliable than the flint-lock.

When combined with improved methods of rifling barrels, more efficient and accurate firearms were available for military use. The muzzle-loading rifle became the standard infantry arm in European and American armies. The range and rate of unit firepower was consequently increased.

A further equipment change was brought about by the widespread and enthusiastic introduction of many sword bayonets which were generally used on carbines. The ubiquitous socket bayonet continued widely in service and was employed, for example, with the Minie rifle of 1851, the Enfield rifle of 1853, and other later patterns. However, the 19th century was notable for sword bayonet research. It was primarily designed 'to combine the functions of sword and pike and thus relieve the infantryman of the short sword, or hanger, which he carried with all his other impediments'[2]. Previously, this sword/hanger 'was adopted as a side arm for infantry and then by specialised troops such as pioneers and riflemen, the latter being adopted to fit as a bayonet'[3].

The sword bayonet was produced in a profusion of differing patterns some of which were rather over ambitious and unnecessarily ostentatious. They were usually robust and effective weapons with hilts fashioned for a hand grip, enabling them to be wielded as a sword when necessary. We now appreciate that the arm was designed as both a sword and a bayonet. Its sword characteristics also sometimes made it useful as a general purpose tool for performing non-military but

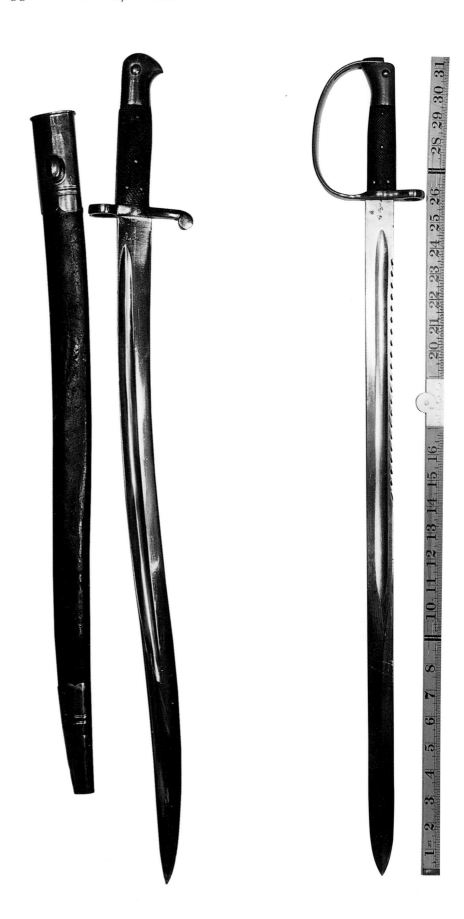

Left:
Sword bayonet for British Enfield Artillery carbine of 1856. Hilt has long, deeply fullered yataghan blade. Steel hilt has chequered cheek plates retained by three rivets. Item complete with leather scabbard tipped with steel locket and chape. The 23-inch blade compensated for the short carbine in bayonet fighting.

Right:
British artillery saw-back sword bayonet to fit Martini Henry carbine and the Snider conversion Enfield (1875-9). Note long, wide fullers for two-thirds of the blade, and the saw-back comprising a double row of teeth.

AUTHOR'S COLLECTION.

essential everyday tasks such as wood chopping. The blades are usually very long, particularly those fitted to carbines; these compensated for the shorter barrels. This was a reflection of the centuries-old tradition of possessing a long hand-weapon which outreached that of an opponent in the close-quarter melee. A rifle fitted with the long bladed sword bayonet enabled a most effective forward lunge in bayonet fighting.

Sword bayonets have either a single- or double-edged blade tapering to a long point. Some are straight, others curved in yataghan form and a few, such as the Elcho, have swelling spear-head shaped blades near the tip. They have a variety of cross guards; these are generally straight, often tipped with circular ends, or forward slanting quillons. Others have circular, or rectangular, knuckle bows providing better hand protection when the arm is used in the sword role. Amongst such patterns as the Brunswick experimental pattern of 1836, the Baker 1st and 2nd sword bayonet patterns, and the Sappers and Miners bayonet of 1841. A few rare items, such as the Naval cutlass bayonet of 1858, have very wide, sword-hilt type curved guards. The quillons and guards would hold or deflect an opponent's blades in bayonet fighting. On some patterns, there is a circular aperture at the top of one guard side to accommodate the rifle muzzle (known as a bayonet ring). Hilts varied considerably, being fashioned from wood, brass, steel, leather or composition. Generally they were straight but occasionally had a raised curve on the bottom side to provide better hand grip. Pommels are often beaked-shaped better to prevent the arm sliding out of the hand. The most common hilt feature is the metal button operating the bayonet attachment locking spring. It should be noted that some sword bayonets, such as the Sappers and Miners bayonet of 1841, have socket hilts.

The French produced a restricted issue sword bayonet in 1842. It comprised a curved, yataghan blade, deeply fullered on both sides, with brass hilt and steel scabbard. It was used with their M1842,

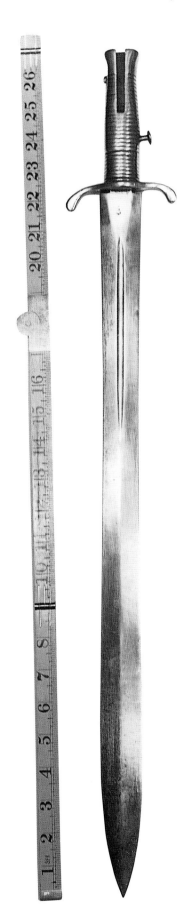

Sword bayonet for British Brunswick rifle pattern 1836. Note straight, double edged blade swelling to form spear head shape towards point and brass guard and hilt. Hilt has deep slot to enable attachment to side of rifle with catch mechanism operated by steel bar topped with button. This pattern was used by Rifle regiments in the Crimean War. Blade length: 22 inches, hilt: length 4.3 inches.

AUTHOR'S COLLECTION.

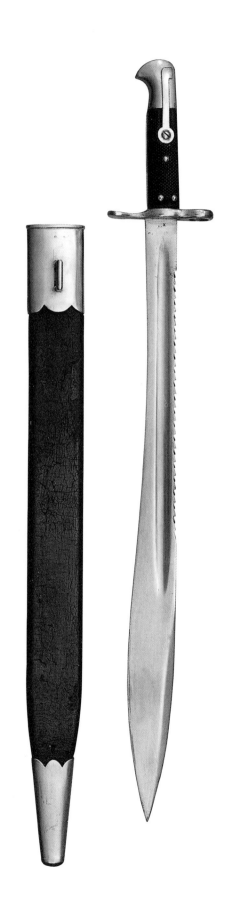

British Elcho saw-backed
sword bayonet and scabbard
of 1871/4 used on the
Martini Henry rifle. Beaked
pommel slotted for rifle bar
and fitted with leaf spring
catch operated by button.
Spear shaped blade with
fullers. Complete with
leather scabbard tipped with
steel locket and chape.
Overall length: 25.3 inches,
blade length: 20 inches.
(NEG NO: A10/147)

BOARD OF TRUSTEES OF
THE ROYAL ARMOURIES.

M1846, and M1853 carbines. These were carried by elite troops and non commissioned officers (NCOs) as a status privilege between 1842 and 1866. Special pattern bayonets were periodically issued by several nations to NCOs as a mark of their seniority. The French bayonet of 1842 is rare and should be immediately purchased by collectors. The subsequent French bayonet of 1866 (used with the Chassepot rifle), and the 1874 pattern (fitted to the Gras rifle) are much more common.

Saw Back Bayonets

Many bayonet patterns were produced with saws on the blade back comprising two rows of teeth. There were several reasons for this. Such bayonets enabled the arm to be used as a saw; it enhanced the intimidating and menacing appearance of the weapon, and the feature was used to indicate the status of non-commissioned officers. For the latter reason the weapon was often only distributed as a limited issue. The Germans produced a saw back version of their long, slim, general issue bayonet for the Mauser rifle GEW 98 of 1898. This was distributed to NCOs on a scale of six per cent to each company. Because such weapons are moderately rare, collectors should acquire them when possible and certainly in preference to those of the same pattern without saw backs issued in much higher numbers to soldiers.

American trowel bayonet of 1873 fitted to the 1873 and 1879 carbines. A curious and unusual item designed to perform dual functions of bayonet and entrenching tool. Doubtless experiences in the later stages of the war between the states prompted its design. Rifle fire power made trench protection essential when fighting on the defensive. Few were actually made. Blade length: 9.8 inches, hilt: 3.5 inches.

AUTHOR'S COLLECTION.

Rare British Sword Bayonets

Some most interesting British bayonet patterns were produced in unusual and rather exotic forms to accompany experimental rifles. Examples of these are: Brunswick (patterns 1836/7), Sappers and Miners (2nd pattern 1843), Jacobs (pattern 1856), Whitworth (1857), Elcho (patterns 1870/1 and 1895), and the Naval Cutlass (1875).

Because several of these, such as the Whitworth rifle bayonet, were produced on a limited experimental basis, whilst others were only in service for short periods, they are rare. Collectors are therefore advised to acquire some of these patterns which remain a good and emotive investment.

Effect of Muzzle-Loading Rifles on the Bayonet

The new rifles were more reliable, accurate, and had longer ranges than the musket. To a degree, therefore, armies could now inflict casualties upon each other from greater distances. In theory this reduced opportunities for bayonets to be used as a killing weapon. In practice, this was not always the case because firearms still used black powder (as did artillery) for ignition purposes which caused battlefields to be partially obscured by smoke. To overcome the problem, protagonists were often compelled to fight at fairly close proximity. This was very evident during the War between the States, in America, where both sides employed, amongst other firearms, the Minie and Enfield rifles, with long-range capability. Because of the conditions described, however, their range potential was often underused enabling the bayonet to retain some close-quarter capability. In Chapter VII, we shall examine how later improved explosive compounds did eventually restrict the bayonet to a close combat role.

One snag of most sword bayonets was the way they slightly unbalanced the rifle fixed to the firearm during firing. This caused marksmanship inaccuracies. It might be thought this problem was irrelevant as soldiers probably used their new, more powerful firearms at long range with the bayonet unfixed. As we know, this was by no means always the case. So, to overcome the problem rifles were re-zeroed with the bayonet fitted.

Notes

1 Logan Thompson, *'The Waterloo Campaign'*, The British Army Review Magazine, August 1967.
2 Charles ffoulkes & E C Hopkinson, *Sword, Lance and Bayonet*, Arco Publishing Company Inc., New York.
3 Howard L Blackmore, *Hunting Weapons*, Barrie & Jenkins, London

*'The Thin Red Line'
The Coldstreamers at the Alma during the Crimean War (from 'Coldstreamers at Alma' by Canton Woodville).*

REPRODUCED BY KIND PERMISSION OF THE REGIMENTAL LIEUTENANT-COLONEL, COMMANDING THE COLDSTREAM GUARDS.

Chapter VII

THE LATE
19TH CENTURY

During this period, powerful, breech loading, magazine equipped, long range rifles became the standard issue firearm of most nations. The successful invention of a breech loading system, plus efficient bolts, had naturally increased the firing rate. Perhaps more important was the later development of the new, powerful and smokeless explosive compounds which replaced black powder. All these improvements usually caused armies to fight battles separated by much greater distances. Infantry ability to cause casualties at much longer ranges consequently restricted bayonet use to occasional close-quarter fighting. This reduced bayonet casualties. The Franco-Prussian War of 1870-1 confirms the trend.

Colonial Wars

There were, of course, regular exceptions to the decline of bayonet combat usage particularly when the colonial powers became embroiled militarily with the consolidation and expansion of their empires. Periodically, they unexpectedly sustained reverses in such wars because the opposition encountered was far more formidable than anticipated. Such conflicts involved, for instance, Spain and France in north Africa; and Great Britain, Germany and Italy in other areas of that continent.

During the Zulu wars a British force was completely overwhelmed by a superior army of Zulus at Isandlwhana (1879). Delay in issuing ammunition was said to have been one cause of the defeat together with a failure to form squares early enough. Thereafter, a tiny mixed British unit was besieged by some 4,000 Zulus at Rorkes Drift. At the climax of this exciting conflict, epitomising true soldiering, the adrenalin pumping, desperate, close-quarter fighting involved rifle (probably unloaded) and bayonet against shield, knob-kerries, and assegai with victory only very narrowly won by supreme guts, courage and determination – a classic example of a battle in which bayonets were essential as a last resort weapon. In 1883, the army of General Hicks Pasha was overwhelmed in the Sudan; whilst in 1896, the Italians, in their attempted conquest of Abyssinia, sustained a humiliating defeat at Adowa. At the battle of Omdurman (1898) the British used machine guns to halt the fast moving cavalry army of the Khalifa. Without them victory would not have been so easily achieved; indeed, it could not have been guaranteed.

One cause of European military defeats, or near defeats against highly mobile and close-combat experienced nomadic peoples was the single shot rifle. Because they could only be loaded with one bullet at a time they had a slow firing rate. So, although their volley fire might initially be effective, if the enemy charge was not convincingly halted, then the Europeans were in trouble. This sometimes enabled a ferocious, brave, highly mobile, battle experienced, nomadic enemy to reach their opponents before they could reload. At this point the bayonet was very useful. However, on such occasions, even with rifles and fixed bayonets, European troops were at a distinct disadvantage because they lacked close-combat experience against a brave, robust, completely ruthless enemy armed with highly tempered spears (both throwing and stabbing) and very high quality swords. Such tribesmen were in their element wielding weapons designed specifically for man-to-man struggles for which they had been well trained. The British army suffered additional problems because of the issue of poor quality bayonets which aggravated infantry problems during 1884/5 in the Sudan Campaigns. These are of direct relevance to bayonet history and are examined in detail under 'Bayonet Problems' (page 98).

Eventually, the magazine was invented which immediately provided a soldier with an ammunition reserve. This comprised a metal box containing a supply of spare bullets which was attached beneath the rifle. An internal spring, which automatically pushed up a fresh round into the breech, meant that the rifle could be immediately re-loaded after the previous spent cartridge case had been discarded by the withdrawal of the bolt. In the Boer War it was soon obvious that the bayonet had become less significant. This was because both sides employed very powerful, long-range rifles fitted with magazines which kept armies, for most of the time, at considerable distances. Bayonet combat use was thus much restricted.

Socket Bayonets

The upsurge of sword bayonet use during this century should not be allowed to obscure the continued employment of socket bayonets. Collectors will be aware that these were used on the following British service firearms: percussion muskets of 1839 and 1842, the Minie rifle of 1851, the Enfield rifle of 1855, and the Snider Enfield breech loading rifle of 1865. The Martini Henry rifle of 1871 had a yataghan bladed sword bayonet; the Lee Metford rifle of 1888, fitted with a magazine, had a shortish, straight, double-edged bayonet with blade of 12.25 inches. The last socket bayonet in the traditional form was a high quality one used with the Martini Enfield rifle of 1895. This has a triangular shaped blade of 21.5 inches. Collectors should acquire these as long as the arm is accompanied by its scabbard.

Before buying socket bayonets collectors should carefully establish the exact pattern of the ones on offer. The author has frequently experienced difficulty in identifying these. It is again recommended that consultation concerning British models be made with *British Military Bayonets*, by R J Wilkinson Latham. Many later socket bayonets are fitted with various fairly intricate forms of locking rings indicating continued concern about the weapon falling off the firearm barrel. Evidently, some patterns still harboured limitations, for instance at the battle of Meanee during the Scinde campaign (1843). According to Sir Sibald Scott, in the Journal of the Royal United Service Institution, 'the men of the 22nd regiment had their bayonets pulled off by the Bellochee enemy and had to tie them on with string and wire'[1].

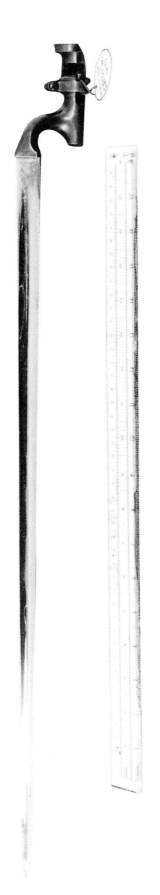

Socket bayonet of 1876 to fit Martini Henry rifle of 1876-87. This pattern supercedes the 1853 Enfield socket bayonet. Item has blued hilt with circular locking ring and narrow fullered blade. Item complete with leather scabbard mounted with brass at chape and locket. This has two brass studs on front side to retain an internal spring which held bayonet firmly in scabbard. Blade length: 21.5 inches, overall: 24.5 inches.

See: 'Bayonet Problems', page 98.

AUTHOR'S COLLECTION.

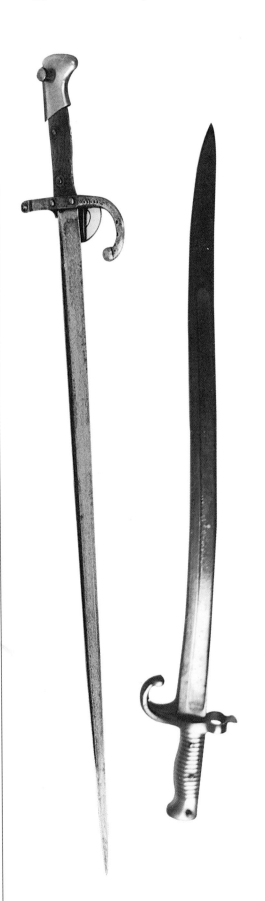

Left:
French bayonet issued for use with the 11mm, single-shot, bolt action Gras rifle M 1874. This item replaced the long, curved sword bayonet of 1866 used on the Chassepot rifle. Blade length: 20.5 inches; hilt: 4.95 inches. A very similar but shorter bayonet was also made for the Gras carbine. This was interchangeable with both rifle and carbine; its overall length was 16.5 inches. These being rarer than the longer bayonet, they should be immediately purchased.

Right:
French sword bayonet to fit the highly efficient Chassepot rifle of 1866. This was a single-shot, needle fire, bolt action military rifle which permitted accurate, long-range fire. The bayonet was far less successful because, if used too vigorously, it bent and distorted the barrel. Overall length: 26.75 inches, blade: 22.5 inches.

AUTHOR'S COLLECTION.

French Bayonets

It is of interest now to examine briefly the bayonets used by the French, an important military nation during this period, because several differed greatly in form from those employed by other countries. Collectors are aware that the French Chassepot rifle of 1866 was issued with a sabre (sword) bayonet with long curved blade, deep fullers, and a brass hand grip fashioned with serrations and leaf spring barrel catch. It was replaced by the Gras rifle in 1874 with its strong T section blade and single swept forward quillon guard. This rifle continued in use until World War I as the arm of French territorial and reserve formations. The Gras carbine had a very similar but much shorter blade of 12 inches. In 1886 (see picture) a very different bayonet was produced, with slender 20.5-inch cruciform blade for use with the Lebel rifle. There were two variations of this model; one had a fixed hilt, and the other a removable one which can be taken off by unscrewing the round retaining nut inset into the end of the hilt. Large numbers were produced and issued to all French units and colonial troops. It was also distributed to the French Foreign Legion. This was to be the principal French bayonet during World War I. Unfortunately, the pattern had a tendency to snap off about 9 inches from the hilt after an awkward thrust. In 1916, a new model, number M 86/93/16, was produced. This was very similar to the 1886 pattern upon which its design is based. The blade is straight and cruciform shaped. There is no quillon but the guard has a squared lower part. Hilts are generally of brass, some of German silver, and very occasionally of steel. The blade length was 20.5 inches. The bayonet was issued with the 8mm Lebel rifle used during World War I. If a collector is lucky he may acquire one complete with its circular metal scabbard and leather belt frog which has a strap and brass buckle passing through the loop on the scabbard.

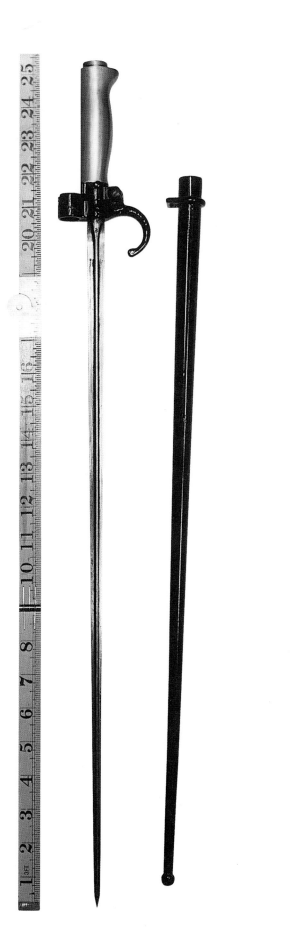

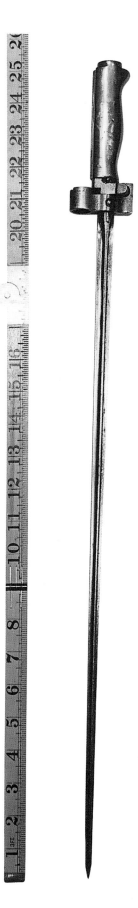

Left:
French epée bayonet model 1886. The long slender blade has a German silver hilt with groove along its back for attachment to the rifle bar. It was issued to all French units, the Foreign Legion and Colonial troops. They were accompanied by a circular metal scabbard with rounded ferrule at tip. Overall length: 24.1 inches, blade: 20.5 inches.

Right:
French bayonet model M 86/93/16. This is very similar to the 1886 pattern except there is no quillon guard. Hilts were of brass or German silver and occasionally steel. The bayonet was used with the 8mm Lebel rifle and semi automatic rifles used in WWI. Item complete with circular metal scabbard. Overall length: 20.5 inches, blade: 3.6 inches.

AUTHOR'S COLLECTION.

Bayonet Problems

We have already noted how the most common bayonet problem was its tendency periodically to drop off the firearm. During the years 1884-5, it suffered far more serious problems. These related to the weapons' metal quality and battle effectiveness. Coincidentally, similar shortcomings arose with swords. Here, we shall concentrate upon the bayonet difficulties. These were: instances of the weapon blade snapping in two, or markedly bending; failure to kill an opponent after one or even two successful thrusts, and the difficulty in retrieving the blade from the body of an adversary. These shortcomings naturally caused considerable alarm, engendering much public discussion and publicity in the national press over an issue which became known as the 'Bayonet scandal of 1885'. Military problems with the bayonet were encountered in the Sudan campaigns of 1884, details of which appeared in newspapers the following year. 'After various reports a committee was appointed under Sir Drury Lowe, who recommended that tests should be increased in severity.'[2]. Problems mostly related to the 1853 sword bayonet and the socket bayonet for the Martini Henry rifle pattern of 1876.

The special correspondent of the *Daily Telegraph*, Mr Burleigh, who accompanied British troops during their advance to Khartoum, wrote a most interesting article on the whole subject. His account was as follows.

'It was at El Tab that I was first struck with the inferior quality of the English bayonet and sword bayonet. I determined before writing about the matter to watch it in use once more. At Tamai, in the rush and scurry, it was put to a severer test than anywhere else in the Sudan. In that battle the Hadendowas, as they rushed out of their grass-cover with their short spears, fairly pitched themselves upon the weapons of our Black Watch and 65th. The triangular bayonet oft-times bent and twisted. On the whole, however, it stood the test better than the sword bayonet, I think. Like the sword bayonet, it often bent like hoop-iron when a thrust was made, if a bone interposed and became cork-screwed in the struggle. It has two serious drawbacks, not so observable in the sword bayonet. The wound it makes is slight, so that a fanatical savage or an infuriated man requires several thrusts before he is placed hors de combat, giving him a chance to run amuck among civilised troops. In the second place, the triangular bayonet, when thrust violently, goes too far, and there is great difficulty in freeing it. At Tamai a stalwart soldier hooked his opponent in such a manner that he had to draw the body twenty yards, as we were retreating, before liberating his weapon. This was the most conspicuous instance of the kind I saw, but it was by no means the only one. The sword bayonet has weight without breadth, and, with the cutlass, frequently lacks temper. I have seen a blue jacket's cutlass and sword bayonet at Tamai, as well as some in the battles up the Nile, bend into a semi-circle, and remain in that shape, unfitting it for a second 'point'. The use it was put to did not justify the giving way of the weapon. The fact that it did not regain its form proved the quality of the blade was of the poorest. What I have said of the bad quality of the cutlass applies equally to the sword bayonet. Many a soldier at Abou Klea saw with dismay his bayonet rendered useless at the moment when there was no chance to load his rifle, and when he most stood in need of its services. There also I saw sword bayonets bend and twist with the facility of soft iron rather than steel. After that fight you might have noticed brawny foot-guardsmen, Herculean life-guardsmen, and the deft fighters of the mounted infantry, all of whom had stood shoulder to shoulder in the square, straighting their bayonets across their knee or under foot. Others there were who discarded their distorted weapons and picked up some dead comrade's from the field.'

The problems were caused by poor metal, low manufacturing standards, and insufficiently rigorous testing. During the final checking process the blades were bend tested and to pass this some bayonets were made unhardened. 'This was necessary because, if hardened, they would break under tests, as inferior steel was used in the manufacture.'[3] The second problem was that bayonets which had been cased hardened lost much of it during the final grinding task, which naturally removed case hardening causing some soft metal to be exposed. However, all these malpractices were eventually abolished. The 1853 sword bayonet and the 1876 socket bayonet were declared obsolete. They were replaced by the much higher quality 1886 sword bayonet fitted to the Martini Henry rifle.

Notes

1 Charles ffoulkes and E C Hopkinson, *Sword, Lance and Bayonet*, Arco Publishing Company Inc., New York.
2, 3 R J Wilkinson Latham, *British Military Bayonets*, Hutchinson.

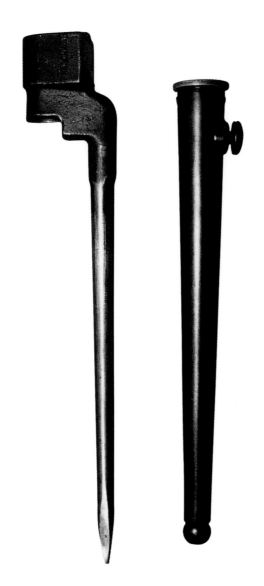

The British Socket Bayonet and circular scabbard, No 4, Mk II, fitted to the .303 Lee Enfield rifle, 1940, called the 'spike' bayonet. Blade: 9ins, total weight: 7oz.

REPRODUCED WITH PERMISSION OF THE MUSEUM OF LANCASHIRE, PRESTON.

Chapter VIII

THE 20TH CENTURY

In this chapter we study the evolution of the bayonet from the end of the 19th century, through both World Wars, up to the present day. It should be noted that sword bayonet use continued into the new century and some were employed during World War I.

In the mid 1880s the major powers had adopted machine guns such as the Maxim and the Vickers. Later, smaller patterns of light machine guns, for example the Lewis, and the French Chauchat 8mm, were introduced. These were to be decisive from 1914 onwards.

On the bayonet front, the British had adopted a new sturdy sword bayonet for use with the short magazine Lee Enfield rifle (1902), which was a shorter version of the 1895 .303 bore Lee Enfield firearm. The new bayonet is longer than the double-edged bladed one used on the Lee Metford with strong, straight, single-edged blade of 12.25 inches, and single hooked quillon guard incorporating a bayonet ring. On later patterns the hooked quillon is omitted.

The Turkish army had a rather interesting bayonet. This comprised a strong, tapering, single-edged blade of 18 inches with both blade sides near the tip ground to a point. Blade sides are fullered for 12 inches and marked with Arabic lettering. The cross guard is robust with one quillon end forming a pronounced forward curved guard ending in a spherical knob. The hilt of 4.5 inches is fashioned with two wooden cheek plates secured by two rivets. This weapon was made in Germany and fitted to the German-produced Turkish 7.65 Mauser of 1890. The pattern will also fit the Turkish Mausers of 1893 and 1903-5.

German Bayonets

It is appropriate now to examine the side arms of Germany, the nation which had the largest regular army in 1914. Collectors know there are always many of these on the market. This is not surprising considering the two major wars in which our nations were embroiled.

We start with the Mauser 11mm single-shot rifle model of 1871, the bullet of which was powered with black powder. This was equipped with a single-edged, deeply fullered bayonet, with raised muzzle ring. The lower blade section is ground to the point on both blade sides. Blade length is 10 inches, the hilt 4.9 inches. The rifle was modified in the 1871/4 pattern by the addition of a magazine. A rarer and more expensively produced bayonet was also used with this rifle, and issued to elite regiments (see picture). This has an 18-inch straight, fullered blade with S-shaped guard and brass hilt. Like the previous bayonet, it is ground on both lower blade sides to form the point. A saw-backed version was issued to NCOs. The brass hilt is particularly noticeable with seventeen diagonal hand grip serrations on one side only. The pommel is in a distinctive eagle beak shape. The steel spring catch mechanism is within the hilt. Such models should be bought on sight. The author's example was made in 1878 by Weyersberg Brothers at Solingen and issued to the 51st Reserve Regiment, a splendid high quality piece with arsenal mark of a crowned Erfurt on the blade flat. The item is contained in a black leather, brass-tipped scabbard.

We progress now to the 7.92 Mauser rifle Model 98, introduced in 1898, which was 'the most successful bolt-action rifle ever produced. In one form or another, the 98 action has been used by most of the countries of the world since 1898.'[1] So, a significant number of relevant bayonets were made for use with this rifle or its variations. The first is in two models: a plain one without a saw back, and a rarer one with a saw back issued to NCOs. The latter comprises two rows of teeth on the top side of the blade. Both patterns are otherwise identical. The blade is 20.5 inches, being the longest ever used on this rifle and extremely narrow, with shallow fullers and slight spear head form towards the tip. It has no bayonet ring but one small guard curved backwards towards the hilt. The hilt of 4.8 inches is made from two separate wooden cheek plates each secured by two rivets. Hand grip is provided by eight grooves cut diagonally on both hilt sides. The item fitted a leather, steel-tipped scabbard. These were used in World War I.

The next was a sword bayonet used on both the Mauser rifle of 1898 Model Gew 98, and the KAR 98 carbine. Again, it was produced in two very similar patterns: one with a saw back the other without. Apart from the blade back, both patterns are almost identical. The blade of 14.5 inches widens from the hilt to form a slightly spear-head shape (reminiscent of the earlier Elcho bayonet). Both blade sides are deeply fullered. The hilt has no bayonet ring but one short quillon curving back towards the hilt. The hilt is almost identical to that on the very long-bladed bayonet previously examined, being made from two wooden cheek plates screwed into position, beaked pommel, and hand grip serrations cut diagonally. This weapon was used widely in Europe and Germany's African colonies. German pioneers only

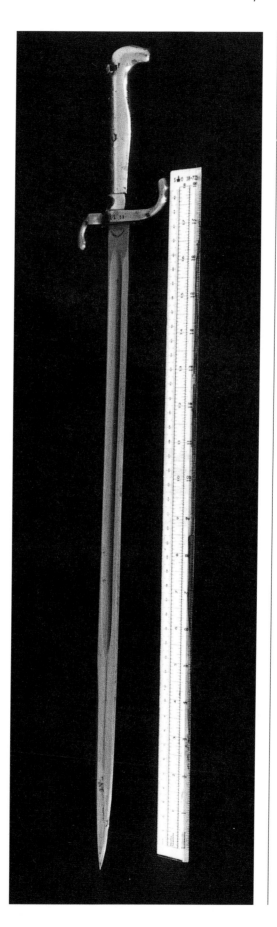

Prussian infantry bayonet fitted to the 11mm, single shot, bolt action Mauser rifle of 1871. This was the first Mauser to be made in production quantities. Straight, single-edged blade but ground towards the tip upon both sides to form point. Both sides fullered for length of 11.75 inches. Brass hilt with seventeen hand grip serrations on one side; pommel in distinctive German eagle-beak form. Steel S-shaped guard. Item complete with black leather scabbard mounted in brass at chape and locket. Pronounced brass clip for attachment to bayonet frog. This item was used by The Hohenzollern Fusiliers, weapon number 242. Overall length: 23 inches, blade: 18 inches.
AUTHOR'S COLLECTION.

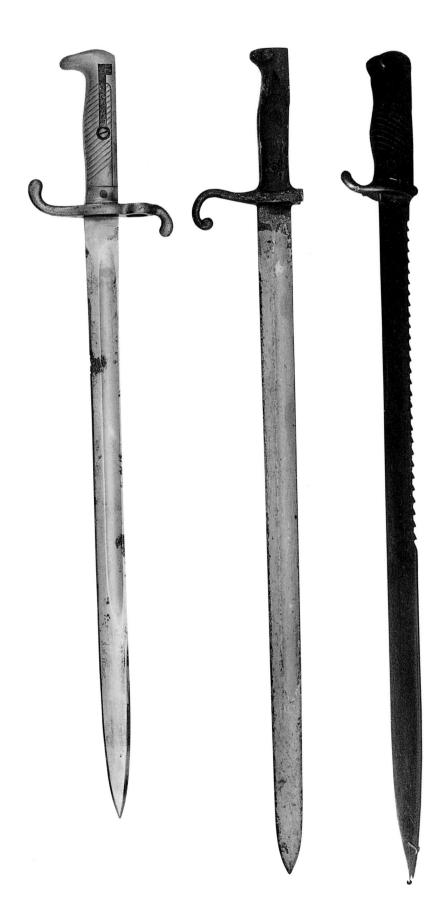

used the saw-back pattern on short rifle (carbine) KAR98 and Mauser GEW98. This had a blade of 25.3 ins. In World War I soldiers employed them to cut through the wooden posts supporting the Allied barbed wire. The Germans strung their wire on steel corkscrew posts. The KAR carbine and its successor the KARa was used in World War I. Early models had leather and steel-tipped scabbards whilst later ones were of steel.

A rather unusual and crude bayonet was produced at the end of World War I for use on the Mauser rifle GEW98. This all-steel weapon is best described as an ersatz issue. It is of considerable interest, despite its utilitarian appearance, because it clearly illustrated the marked decline in weapon manufacturing standards caused by acute shortages of raw materials in Germany towards the end of the war. The blade of 14.25 inches is straight, with single cutting edge except towards the tip where both blade sides are ground to form the tip. There is a raised open-top bayonet ring. The hilt of 4.45 inches is of plain steel, flat at the top but roughly shaped as a hand grip on the underside. The hilt catch mechanism comprises a circular button which releases a rectangular shaped locking piece. The item was issued with all steel scabbard constructed of two thin pieces of metal with the top section bent over the lower and pressed to form seal.

Left:
German Mauser bayonet model 1871.
Centre:
Sword bayonet Mauser 1898, converted from Vetterli.
(NEG NOS X350, X351)
THE BOARD OF TRUSTEES OF THE ROYAL ARMOURIES

Right:
German saw-back version of bayonet fitted to the Mauser rifle GEW 98. These were issued to NCOs, whilst the plain version (without saw-back) was issued in much larger numbers to soldiers. This was equipped with leather scabbard mounted in steel at locket and chape. Item was used during WWI. Overall length: 25.3 inches, blade: 20.5 inches.
AUTHOR'S COLLECTION.

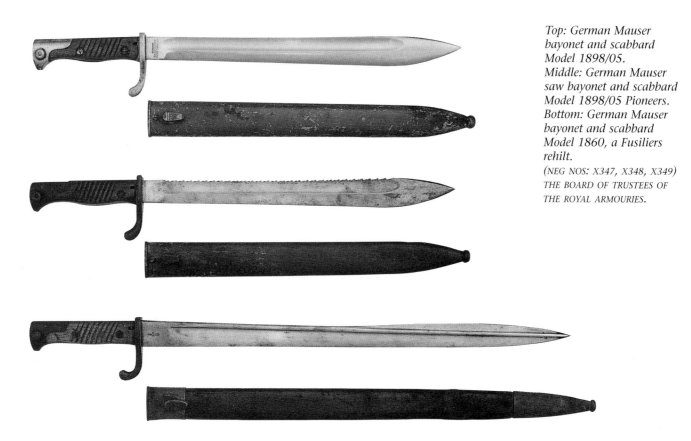

Top: German Mauser bayonet and scabbard Model 1898/05.
Middle: German Mauser saw bayonet and scabbard Model 1898/05 Pioneers.
Bottom: German Mauser bayonet and scabbard Model 1860, a Fusiliers rehilt.
(NEG NOS: X347, X348, X349)
THE BOARD OF TRUSTEES OF THE ROYAL ARMOURIES.

Coldstream Guardsmen at the battle of the Alma during the Crimean War were equipped with Enfield muzzle loading, percussion operated rifles of 1853 with socket bayonets incorporating locking rings.
REPRODUCED BY THE KIND PERMISSION OF THE REGIMENTAL LIEUTENANT COLONEL, COMMANDING THE COLDSTREAM GUARDS.

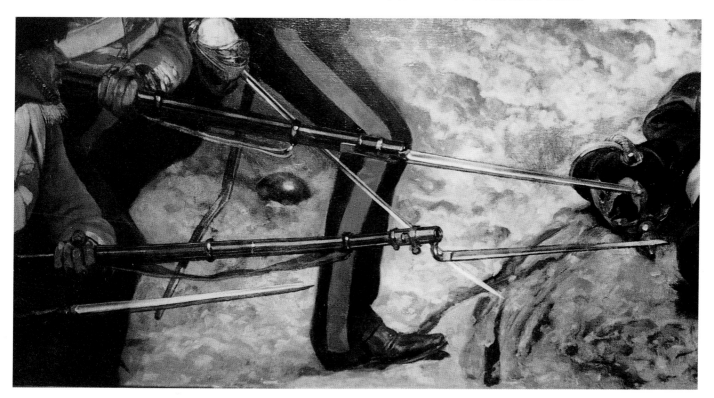

The First World War

By the 20th century the bayonet was certainly no longer a battle-winning weapon. Nonetheless, it was still regarded as a most useful piece of equipment. Infantry soldiers of all nations went to war for the most part equipped with rifle and bayonet, some of which were of the sword type. It is of great interest that, despite some awareness of machine gun effectiveness, leading combatants failed to appreciate that a weapon so effective against the natives and tribesmen might, perhaps, be just as devastating against Europeans. Instead, the prevailing and over-optimistic, nationalistic opinion was that courage, elan and the bayonet would somehow achieve victory over other nations equipped with medium machine guns. This misplaced resurgence of the bayonet's importance was rapidly to have serious consequences. French troops were sent into battle enthused with an excess of patriotism, misplaced confidence, and colourful uniforms, and suffered some 350,000 casualties in about four months. Later, the British suffered a similar fate on the Somme where, despite lengthy and massive artillery bombardments, our army sustained some 450,000 casualties in about four and a half months. The Russians and Austrians also suffered heavy losses. These experiences provided the very sad high point of the bayonets' history. Nonetheless, it remained a means of maintaining good morale. The machine gun was probably responsible for causing more casualties than any other weapon in the history of warfare!

Eventually, on the Western Front at least, a horrific stalemate of trench warfare developed. Bayonet status and credibility was reduced to more realistic levels. If a unit could reach the opposing trenches in adequate numbers it was most useful in the close-quarter fighting. Conversely, if the enemy managed to infiltrate one's own sector it was an effective hand-to-hand means of repelling them. Other implements were adapted for use in these circumstances, such as the trench knife, clubs, and spades honed on one edge to a high degree of sharpness.

Between the World Wars

After the war, the Germans undertook a detailed appreciation of the reasons for their defeat. This was particularly relevant to them because their new army was restricted in size to only 100,000 men. To compensate for small numbers it was therefore essential that all their equipment was the best. They realised their Mauser rifle was too powerful and over-ranged. A new one, the Mauser M 98 k Carbine was introduced in 1935. Detailed research was also undertaken on a novel automatic rifle which was eventually issued as the revolutionary Sturmgewehr assault rifle in 1944. The bayonet was relegated to the status of an auxiliary weapon and a new, smaller pattern was produced. This fitted the new rifle and the Mauser GEW 98. The short blade of 9.8 inches is fullered, blued and single-edged. The top-edged side of the blade, near the hilt, is flattened, unlike that on the M84/98 bayonet where it was rounded. The hilt of 4.9 inches is constructed of red composition cheek plates retained with steel screws. Cheek plates have hand grip serrations. This neat and functional arm is carried in a steel scabbard. It is worthy of mention that German weapon research resulted in two exceptional automatic weapons. These were: a sub machine gun, the MP 38, and subsequent modified patterns of 40 and 41; and the machine guns 34 and 42.

Two soldiers of the Argyll and Sutherland Highlanders at the battle of Lys in May 1918. They both have short magazine Lee Enfield rifles fitted with 17-inch long 1917 pattern sword bayonets.
(NEG NO: Q6617)
IMPERIAL WAR MUSEUM.

The British also undertook an appreciation of the bayonet. This revealed that the sword bayonet (used on the S. M. L. E.) was too long, heavy and cumbersome 'and that a man with a short handy weapon will beat an equally skilled man with a long cumbersome weapon practically every time'[2]. Furthermore, 'the utility of the bayonet as a cutlass or dagger proved to be negligible, hence the demand for trench knives, clubs, etc'[3]. A final point which emerged was one fully appreciated by the Germans and doubtless other nations. This was that, for killing purposes, a much shorter blade was perfectly adequate whilst having the additional advantage of being much easier to retrieve. Hence the new German bayonet used with the Mauser with its 9.8-inch blade. In Great Britain, a new socket bayonet was eventually adopted; 'the spike bayonet No4, Mk1 was officially approved on 15 November 1939. The 9-inch blade of which was cruciform in section.'[4]. 'This was too inconspicuous to have the morale effect of the sword bayonet, was an eyesore on ceremonial occasions, and of little use for the multifarious useful, if illegitimate purposes.'[5] Fortunately, this was replaced in 1944 with an 8-inch bladed sword bayonet, model No 6, which was used with the short magazine Lee Enfield rifle.

After World War II

After the war the bayonet was regarded by most nations as being unimportant, and its retention was rather an anachronism. However, its use continued because it was still considered to have some value. It maintained morale, gave soldiers a feeling of extra confidence, and had some potential as a last resort weapon when ammunition was exhausted. It was thus carried by British soldiers during the numerous small wars in which the nation has been involved since 1945. In a few of these it was periodically useful as combat arm, particularly in Korea.

Appreciation of Bayonet Effectiveness Today

This is an appropriate moment to examine the various relevant factors to determine whether or not the weapon should be retained in military service today. The factors studied are: combat effectiveness; morale; general duty functions; and weight.

The short sword bayonet used on the British 7.62 self-loading rifle. A good combat weapon with its 'sheath-knife' blade that could be used when necessary as a trench knife. Picture taken in 1976.
ARMY PUBLIC RELATIONS

Combat Effectiveness

We have seen that the proliferation of automatic weapons (particularly machine guns) has increased firepower to the extent that the potential of the bayonet for inflicting casualties is now theoretically very small. However, even modern wars involving the most sophisticated weapons, for instance in the Gulf, still include tiny instances of bloody, desperate, close-quarter fighting in which personal courage, guts, and physical fitness determine the outcome. On these occasions a soldier will use any weapon which comes to hand, including the bayonet. Such struggles are the modern equivalent of that at Rorkes Drift, and these will undoubtedly periodically occur in all future conflicts.

We have touched upon the problems which a fixed bayonet can cause to firearm accuracy due to the point of balance of the rifle being altered which causes shots to go low. Loss of accuracy is further aggravated by the change of air flow pressure at the muzzle. Therefore, if the bayonet is to be retained, rifles should be zeroed with the bayonet fixed before combat shooting.

Morale

The possession of a bayonet does give a soldier a psychological feeling of greater confidence and fosters the killing instinct. The ownership of an extra weapon, albeit a small one, helps to maintain morale. During internal security situations the actual process of fixing bayonets can have a sobering effect upon an unruly local population intent upon murder and mayhem. Better to resolve such incidents by this gesture than escalating matters by opening fire. Such circumstances have been confronted by the British army on countless occasions since 1945. Experience shows that the glitter of fixed bayonets undoubtedly gives the impression that soldiers mean business.

General Duty Functions

The weapon had always been periodically used on non-military tasks such as wood chopping and cooking. This was markedly so in the sword bayonet era. However, the development of shorter models reduced its usefulness in this respect. Since Word War II its value for these has been exaggerated. It would be a more useful arm if its design incorporated more fully the characteristics of an efficient 'Bowie' type trench knife.

Weight

The less equipment a soldier carries the less fatigued he becomes when marching, or deploying across country. This factor should always be kept in mind. However, the modern scabbard and bayonet weighs only about 17 ounces, thus making little difference to a soldier if dispensed with. Perhaps, if other equipment items were simultaneously discarded, the total weight saving might be significant. As this is unlikely, there is little purpose in discarding the weapon on the grounds of weight.

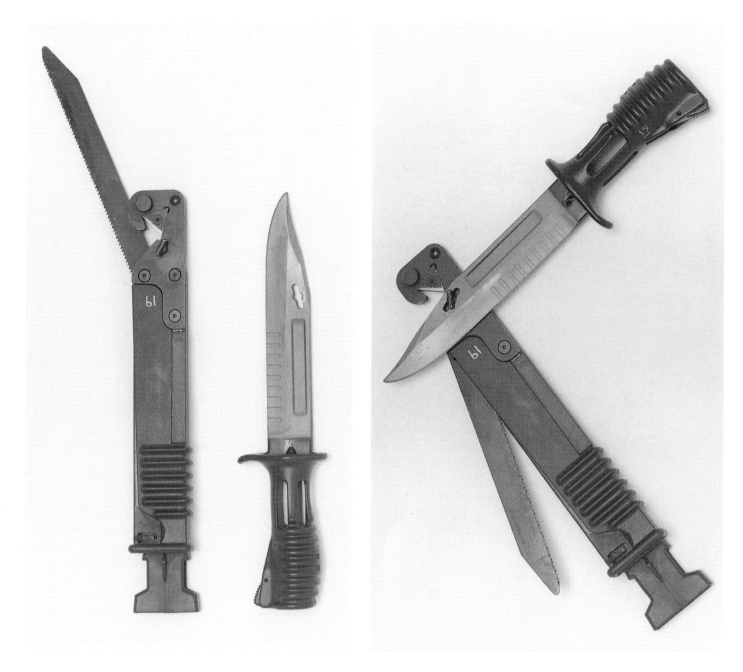

Left
Bayonet for the British SA 80 rifle. Note the rectangular honing device (sharpening stone) at the centre of right side of scabbard; and the hook at the scabbard end which can be used as bottle opener.

Right:
The short contemporary bayonet for the British 5.56mm SA 80 rifle. Note ways in which both scabbard and bayonet are used for additional tasks. The saw blade is partly open, whilst bayonet blade slot is in the ready position for wire cutting. It is the wedge on the blade back together with the hardened surface of the scabbard that provides the effective cutting device.

COURTESY OF THE CURATOR OF THE WEAPONS COLLECTION AT HQ SMALL ARMS SCHOOL CORPS.

Deductions

Let us summarise the contemporary pros and cons of bayonet retention. As a combat weapon its value is almost negligible due to the large scale employment of automatic firearms. However, it could be significant in small, localised, periodic emergencies, and last resort situations when ammunition has run out. Also, its appearance during internal security operations can still calm and deter the development of more serious events. Above all, its possession by soldiers raises and maintains morale. It is rarely used to perform non-military tasks; and the tiny benefit of dispensing with it to save weight is irrelevant. It could be a more useful item if design changes incorporated general purpose service gadgets, and new blade, perhaps fashioned in a Bowie style, which furnished a really effective trench knife.

In conclusion, the bayonet still has a modest function to perform in the modern army and there is no doubt that a soldier equipped with one is slightly more capable of fulfilling his role.

The Present British Army Bayonet

Leading armies today, who generally agree with the above conclusion, are still employing the bayonet. The British army is equipped with one used on the contemporary 5.56 rifle, the SA 80. This is a practical and novel weapon with ingenious design features incorporating several multi-purpose gadgets. The short bladed arm is on the sword type carried in a scabbard on a frog normally attached to the belt or ammunition pouch. The blade shape is scientifically fashioned to achieve successful and rapid close-quarter combat success in bayonet fighting. The scabbard is designed to provide valuable additional gadgets. These are: a saw blade which cuts wood, a sharpening/honing stone, wire cutters operated in conjunction with a slot in the bayonet blade, and bottle opener sited near the scabbard base (see pictures). The wire cutter will deal with both British standard barbed wire and the European 'ribbon' form of wire. This most useful, versatile implement will thus maintain the very long tradition of famous bayonet usage in the British army into the 21st century.

Notes

1   E Clinton Ezell, *Small Arms of the World* (with revisions by W H B Smith), Stackpole Books, Harrisburg.
2, 3, 4 R J Wilkinson Latham, *British Military Bayonets*, Hutchinson.
5   Colonel H B Rogers OBE, *Weapons of the British Soldier,* Seeley Service & Co. Ltd.

Part III
COLLECTION, RENOVATION AND CONSERVATION

A German knightly sword about AD1150-1200, found near Cologne. Brazil nut-shaped pommel; straight quillons square in section, and short tang without grip. The double-edged blade has shallow fuller on both sides and tapers to a point now rounded and pitted by corrosion. Swords like this are still being discovered and sold at auction, often in their excavated condition.

(ACC NO: 457)
THE WALLACE COLLECTION

What to Collect

Old weapon collecting is a popular hobby with some new enthusiasts periodically joining the ranks of their more experienced colleagues. The aim of this section is to assist collectors, particularly those just starting, to develop a dagger, bayonet or any other weapon collection and then conserve it correctly.

The first step is to decide what types of arms to amass. It is only too easy to accumulate a number of disconnected items without theme or purpose. It is, therefore, recommended that a main subject be selected. This could eventually provide the considerable satisfaction of owning a part-set of one weapon type, for example, to concentrate upon acquiring a number of small, percussion pistols of the period 1830 to 1850. After achieving this fairly difficult, but stimulating task, the collector will be rewarded by a sense of satisfaction and a small collection of some significance and historical interest. With patience and perseverance the amateur can achieve such an aim. An accumulation of arms showing the evolution of one type will be especially important. Such a selective collecting method should not, however, deter the acquisition of a rare and fine item of a different category if one appears. The author still regrets failing to purchase, some forty years ago, a Cossack sword mounted in engraved solid silver; it was cheap too! Acquired items which do not equate to your main collection can always be used later as swaps in exchange for one that does, or be sold, hopefully at a profit. This will naturally enable reinvestment in a more appropriate piece.

Where can Arms be Acquired?

The collector has six possible sources. These are: personal acquaintances, relatives, arms dealers who periodically send out sales catalogues, arms fairs, auction houses, and antique shops/markets. They should all be networked. Those whose forebears served in past campaigns may possess appropriate souvenirs and be able to tell interesting stories about them. Authenticated written accounts, which establish a weapon's provenance, can greatly enhance a weapon's value and historical interest. Currently, the number of good available items on the market seems to be declining somewhat. This is possibly due to the large number of collectors, at home and overseas, and greater awareness of antique values. Shortages are periodically offset by the sales, and subsequent break up, of major collections. These instances help to reinvigorate the market. Collectors are advised, incidentally, not to be inhibited from buying at major auction house sales. They can provide opportunities to acquire some most interesting items at acceptably reasonable prices. For instance, Christie's recently sold inexpensively a Swiss knife-dagger of about 1450 in good excavated condition. Such establishments can also provide accurate item advice and price estimates for both sales and purchases.

A collector should consider, when being offered an item which he has long sought, that the buying opportunity may not arise again for many years. Without advocating extravagance, an immediate purchase is recommended. Such action can rightly be excused as a good investment! The author particularly recommends attendance at arms fairs where many dealers are congregated under one roof. This much increases buying opportunities, choice, and price comparisons. Furthermore, they are excellent places in which to learn much about weapons generally. Regular liaison should be established with several dealers many of whom are often most helpful. They should be made aware of your requirements, and of ways of contacting you if and when they locate an item which you seek. Finally, on purchasing an item, the collector should receive from the dealer a signed, detailed invoice. This proof of authenticity and acquisition will enable the collector to insure the weapon.

Identification

When lucky enough to buy a particularly rare and fine weapon do not attempt any renovation until its origin, age, and decoration have been checked. The vendor may enlighten you on its provenance; reference books could clarify further details. If still uncertain as to the precise item details, refrain from any renovation and liaise instead with an expert. Those at museums, or auction houses, will be pleased to help and give free and accurate advice upon item identification. They may also provide excellent tips on the best renovation methods. It is always wise, however, to liaise first with such experts and make an appointment to meet them at a mutually convenient time.

Renovation and Conservation

Once acquired, an item should not necessarily be renovated so that it closely resembles its original state. This is because the dark patination of age, though technically not 'original', deserves to be retained. This is often very pleasing to the eye whilst clearly indicating genuine age.

Many fine firearms and edged weapons possess expensively engraved, decorated, or damascened surfaces perhaps obscured by dirt, rust or decay. This fine work must be very carefully cleaned then preserved. Before doing any cleaning, therefore, always liaise with an expert in order to discover how this delicate task should be undertaken. Common errors are: removal of blueing or browning on firearms and the subsequent polishing of steel. The author has occasionally been offered old edged weapons that have been cleaned on an industrial buffer which has removed genuine patina (and even parts of engraved blade markings!) and replaced them with a dazzling glossy surface. Areas which the buffer could not reach have been left untouched. It is very sad to see the partial ruination of a once rather fine and fairly valuable blade.

We shall now examine how best to renovate the various substances most regularly encountered in weapons.

Woodwork

This is usually found on firearms, hilts of edged weapons such as those on daggers and bayonets, and scabbard liners. Collectors are reminded that, before doing anything, they should heed the advice given to them by an expert. If woodwork renovation is required it is best carefully to remove it from the weapon. Nuts retaining cheek and butt plates can be more easily taken off if first soaked with a little light penetrating oil. Take care to prevent this staining the wood. The nuts should be removed with caution to avoid damage to them or scratching of the wood. The sections taken off may then reveal metal underneath which also needs treatment (see metal section). If wood is very badly stained, or rough, rub down with very fine glass paper, then stain and polish. Generally, it should only be necessary to wash woodwork with a little white spirit and restore its colour with wax polish. Patterned and carved woodwork, which tends to collect dirt, is best gently cleaned with a soft bristle toothbrush. Bristle is preferable to nylon. Many daggers have wooden hilts. If the item has been recovered from a river bottom the woodwork will probably need to be expertly conserved in a museum. Without specialist treatment it will disintegrate.

Metal

If the arm is of fine quality, or great age, do nothing until you have sought expert advice. You may then possibly decide it is better to do no renovation, particularly if the surface has a fine patina. This rule applies to both good quality swords and decorated firearms.

We all appreciate that rust attacks iron and steel because metal iron atoms are adversely affected by moisture. 'Chemicals in the air, acidic materials, or chemicals on human skin, cause atoms to combine with oxygen, hydro-oxide, chlorine and sulphur ions to produce electro-chemical corrosion.'[1]

With modern weapons, such as 19th-century swords and bayonets, the metal of which is undecorated, first soak in light oil them remove rust using oil soaked fine (0000) grade wire wool. If rust is heavily encrusted it may be necessary to resort to 'wet and dry' paper moving from coarse to fine papers, again lubricated with oil. Only in desperation should unlubricated abrasive papers be used. The combination of this abrasive paper and oil simultaneously achieves rust removal and polishing. Once completely rust free, the shiny surface must be protected from dust, air, damp, etc. Therefore, the surface must be shielded. Firearms may have to be re-blued or re-browned. Weapon handling over the years does cause some sections of this original protective finish to be worn away, particularly the gun muzzle and trigger guard. Blueing kits can be procured from gunsmiths. Untreated metal can be protected with oil but this tends to run in warm surroundings and attract dirt; petroleum jelly collects dust. For items without scabbards and engraving better to use a clear varnish which is rather like nail varnish applied with a brush, or spray, after the metal has been given a final clean with de-greasing fluid (e.g acetone or nail varnish remover). Do make sure that all sections of surface have been varnished; it is easy to miss little areas. Possibly the best preserving compound, popular in museums, is a micro-crystalline wax such as Renaissance wax polish made by Picreator. Inner sections of firearms should be lightly oiled. Handling weapons can cause them damage so collectors should wear cotton or rubber gloves: 'as the acids and salts which naturally form on skin can form a rusty fingerprint which etches into the object's surface'[2].

Leather

This material, in various qualities, is often encountered in belts, cross straps, holsters, scabbards, sheaths, Prussian helmets, and rifle slings. Frequently it is hard and unyielding. First, remove any paint with a tiny amount of turpentine, then wash and soften the surface with saddle soap. If leather is very hard refresh it with neat's foot oil and repeat the process the next day. This effective preparation which is obtained from the feet of oxen, can be bought in good hardware shops or saddlers. Failing that rub in black or dark tan polish (to match the original leather colour) with a little fresh water. Rub in fairly firmly, in a series of small circles constantly repeating the process with more polish and fresh water. When a slight shine appears leave the remaining polish to harden, but don't polish it off. It is amazing to see how these processes revive leather fairly quickly. Stitching, the weak spot of leather items, should be gently brushed with a bristle toothbrush, then soaked with polish (quite a lot) and water mix, and left for at least two days. Poor treatment, or neglect of leather, explains why so many swords, bayonets and daggers over 100 years old lack scabbards. Buff leather, frequently used in protective coats during the English Civil War period, waist belts, and suede surfaces are generally best carefully brushed and left alone.

Firearms

If possible, firearms should be displayed in an area which is not prone to major changes in temperature and humidity. Sunlight, particularly direct, must also be avoided. Avoid touching them with bare hands. 'The greatest threat to them, however, comes from inappropriate cleaning and storage. These are factors which you can directly control to protect your collection.'[3] With regard to fine firearms it is reaffirmed that expert advice should always be sought concerning renovation. It if can be arranged, it might be best/safer for the appropriate repair work to be undertaken by an expert.

Collection Records

It is recommended that collectors maintain a collection register. When a new item is acquired it should be given a collection register number. Then it is allocated one complete register page. The required headings on this are: nationality, collection number, section number (for instance, No 4 in the German bayonet sub section), pattern number of arm if it has one (this is particularly relevant with fire arms), date/place of purchase, and purchase price. Each complete section should be categorised by country, form of weapon (for example, sword, pistol, or bayonet etc.). The greater part of the register page is devoted to describing the item. These details emerge during your research process and must only be entered when you are convinced of their accuracy. Specifications for edged weapons are entered at the page bottom as follows: overall length, blade length, and hilt length. Specifications for other arm forms are obviously appropriate to that type. Any additional features must also be entered separately. For example, if a pistol is cased, the box and its contents should be listed and described.

Each collection piece should be immediately identifiable. This is achieved by attaching to each item a round, white, cardboard, metal-edged disc showing the collection number on one side, and section reference number on the other with very short description, e.g. German sword bayonet.

Notes

1, 2, 3 Department of Conservation, Colonial Williamsburg Foundation.

FURTHER READING

Blackmore, Howard L, *Hunting Weapons*, Barrie & Jenkins.

Blackmore, Howard L, *British Military Firearms, 1650-1850*, Herbert Jenkins.

ffoulkes, Charles & Hopkinson, E C, *Sword, Lance and Bayonet*, Arco Publishing

Mann, Sir James KVCO, FBA, *The Wallace Collection Catalogue Part II, European Arms & Armour.*

Montgomery of Alamein, *A History of Warfare*, Collins.

Oakeshott, Ewart, *European Weapons & Armour,* Lutterworth Press.

Peterson, Harold L, *Daggers & Fighting Knives of the Western World*, Barrie & Jenkins.

Wallace, John, *Scottish Swords & Dirks*, Stackpole Books.

Ward Perkins, A B and Wheeler, R E M, *The Museum of London Catalogues.*

Wilkinson, Frederick, *Edged Weapons.*

Wilkinson Latham, R J, *British Military Bayonets*, Hutchinson.

INDEX

(illustration references in bold type)

Index compilation: Miss S K Thompson